LITERACY TEACHER'S EDITION

English No Problem!

Elizabeth Minicz
William Rainey Harper College
Palatine, IL

Marcia L. Taylor
Bernard Kleiman JobLink Learning Center
ISPAT Inland Steel, Inc.
East Chicago, IN

New Readers Press

English—No Problem!™
English—No Problem! Literacy Teacher's Edition
ISBN 1-56420-350-6

Copyright © 2004 New Readers Press
New Readers Press
Division of ProLiteracy Worldwide
1320 Jamesville Avenue, Syracuse, New York 13210
www.newreaderspress.com

All rights reserved. No part of this book may be reproduced or transmitted in any form or by any means, electronic or mechanical, including photocopying, recording, or by any information storage and retrieval system, without permission in writing from the publisher.

Printed in the United States of America
9 8 7 6 5 4 3 2

All proceeds from the sale of New Readers Press materials support literacy programs in the United States and worldwide.

Acquisitions Editor: Paula L. Schlusberg
Developer: Mendoza and Associates
Project Director: Roseanne Mendoza
Project Editor: Pat Harrington-Wydell
Content Editor: Rose DeNeve
Production Director: Heather Witt-Badoud
Designer: Kimbrly Koennecke
Cover Design: Kimbrly Koennecke
Cover Photography: Robert Mescavage Photography

Authors

Elizabeth Minicz
William Rainey Harper College
Palatine, IL

Marcia L. Taylor
Bernard Kleiman JobLink
Learning Center
ISPAT Inland Steel, Inc.
East Chicago, IN

Contributors

National Council Members
Audrey Abed, *San Marcos Even Start Program, San Marcos, TX*
Myra K. Baum, *New York City Board of Education (retired), New York, NY*
Kathryn Hamilton, *Elk Grove Adult and Community Education, Sacramento, CA*
Brigitte Marshall, *Oakland Adult Education Programs, Oakland, CA*
Teri McLean, *Florida Human Resources Development Center, Gainesville, FL*
Alan Seaman, *Wheaton College, Wheaton, IL*

Reviewers
Sabrina Budasi-Martin, *William Rainey Harper College, Palatine, IL*
Linda Davis-Pluta, *Oakton Community College, Des Plaines, IL*
Patricia DeHesus-Lopez, *Center for Continuing Education, Texas A&M University, Kingsville, TX*
Gail Feinstein Forman, *San Diego City College, San Diego, CA*
Carolyn Harding, *Marshall High School Adult Program, Falls Church, VA*
Trish Kerns, *Old Marshall Adult Education Center, Sacramento City Unified School District, Sacramento, CA*
Lydia Omori, *William Rainey Harper College, Palatine, IL*
Debe Pack-Garcia, *Manteca Adult School, Humbolt, CA*
Pamela Patterson, *Seminole Community College, Sanford, FL*
Catherine Porter, *Adult Learning Resource Center, Des Plaines, IL*
Jean Rose, *ABC Adult School, Cerritos, CA*
Eric Rosenbaum, *Bronx Community College Adult Program, Bronx, NY*
Laurie Shapero, *Miami-Dade Community College, Miami, FL*
Terry Shearer, *North Harris College Community Education, Houston, TX*
Abigail Tom, *Durham Technical Community College, Chapel Hill, NC*
Darla Wickard, *North Harris College Community Education, Houston, TX*

Pilot Teachers
Connie Bateman, *Gerber Adult Education Center, Sacramento, CA*
Jennifer Bell, *William Rainey Harper College, Palatine, IL*
Marguerite Bock, *Chula Vista Adult School, Chula Vista, CA*
Giza Braun, *National City Adult School, National City, CA*
Sabrina Budasi-Martin, *William Rainey Harper College, Palatine, IL*
Wong-Ling Chew, *Citizens Advice Bureau, Bronx, NY*
Renee Collins, *Elk Grove Adult and Community Education, Sacramento, CA*
Rosette Dawson, *North Harris College Community Education, Houston, TX*
Kathleen Edel, *Elk Grove Adult and Community Education, Sacramento, CA*
Margaret Erwin, *Elk Grove Adult and Community Education, Sacramento, CA*
Teresa L. Gonzalez, *North Harris College Community Education, Houston, TX*
Fernando L. Herbert, *Bronx Adult School, Bronx, NY*

Carolyn Killean, *North Harris College Community Education, Houston, TX*
Elizabeth Minicz, *William Rainey Harper College, Palatine, IL*
Larry Moore, *Long Beach Adult School, Long Beach, CA*
Lydia Omori, *William Rainey Harper College, Palatine, IL*
Valsa Panikulam, *William Rainey Harper College, Palatine, IL*
Kathryn Powell, *William Rainey Harper College, Palatine, IL*
Alan Reiff, *NYC Board of Education, Adult and Continuing Education, Bronx, NY*
Brenda M. Rodriguez, *San Marcos Even Start, San Marcos, TX*
Juan Carlos Rodriguez, *San Marcos Even Start, San Marcos, TX*
Joan Siff, *NYC Board of Education, Adult and Continuing Education, Bronx, NY*
Susie Simon, *Long Beach Adult School, Long Beach, CA*
Gina Tauber, *North Harris College, Houston, TX*
Diane Villanueva, *Elk Grove Adult and Community Education, Sacramento, CA*
Dona Wayment, *Elk Grove Adult and Community Education, Sacramento, CA*
Weihua Wen, *NYC Board of Education, Adult and Continuing Education, Bronx, NY*
Darla Wickard, *North Harris College Community Education, Houston, TX*
Judy Wurtz, *Sweetwater Union High School District, Chula Vista, CA*

Focus Group Participants
Leslie Jo Adams, *Laguna Niguel, CA*
Fiona Armstrong, *New York City Board of Education, New York, NY*
Myra K. Baum, *New York City Board of Education (retired), New York, NY*
Gretchen Bitterlin, *San Diego Unified School District, San Diego, CA*
Patricia DeHesus-Lopez, *Center for Continuing Education, Texas A&M University, Kingsville, TX*
Diana Della Costa, *Worksite ESOL Programs, Kissimmee, FL*
Frankie Dovel, *Orange County Public Schools, VESOL Program, Orlando, FL*
Marianne Dryden, *Region 1 Education Service Center, Edinburgh, TX*
Richard Firsten, *Lindsay Hopkins Technical Center, Miami, FL*
Pamela S. Forbes, *Bartlett High School, Elgin, IL*
Kathryn Hamilton, *Elk Grove Adult and Community Education, Sacramento, CA*
Trish Kerns, *Old Marshall Adult Education Center, Sacramento City Unified School District, Sacramento, CA*
Suzanne Leibman, *The College of Lake County, Grayslake, IL*
Patty Long, *Old Marshall Adult Education Center, Sacramento City Unified School District, Sacramento, CA*
Brigitte Marshall, *Oakland Adult Education Programs, Oakland, CA*
Bet Messmer, *Santa Clara Adult School, Santa Clara, CA*
Patricia Mooney, *New York State Board of Education, Albany, NY*
Lee Ann Moore, *Salinas Adult School, Salinas, CA*
Lynne Nicodemus, *San Juan Adult School, Carmichael, CA*
Pamela Patterson, *Seminole Community College, Sanford, FL*
Eric Rosenbaum, *Bronx Community College, Bronx, NY*
Linda Sasser, *Alhambra District Office, Alhambra, CA*
Federico Salas, *North Harris College Community Education, Houston, TX*
Alan Seaman, *Wheaton College, Wheaton, IL*
Kathleen Slattery, *Salinas Adult School, Salinas, CA*
Carol Speigl, *Center for Continuing Education, Texas A&M University, Kingsville, TX*
Edie Uber, *Santa Clara Adult School, Santa Clara, CA*
Lise Wanage, *CASAS, Phoenix, AZ*

Contents

Scope and Sequence..viii
About This Series...1
    Meeting Adult Learners' Needs with English—No Problem!..................1
    Series Themes...1
    English—No Problem! Series Components......................................1
    Addressing the Standards..2
    About the Student Books..2
    Assessment...3
    About the Literacy Level Student Book Units................................4
    Teaching Effectively with English—No Problem! Literacy Level.............5
    Tried-and-True Techniques and Games for Literacy Level Learners..........7

Warm-Up Unit A: Cecile's Day.....................................10
♦ Uppercase letters • Numbers 0–10

Lesson 1	In the Parking Lot..................................	11
Lesson 2	At the Office.......................................	12
Lesson 3	At Home..	13
Lesson 4	At the Pharmacy....................................	14
Lesson 5	In the Parking Lot Again...........................	15

Warm-Up Unit B: Omar's Day......................................16
♦ Lowercase letters • Colors

Lesson 1	At Home..	17
Lesson 2	At School..	18
Lesson 3	At the Video Store.................................	19
Lesson 4	In the Office Supply Store.........................	20
Lesson 5	At the Used Car Lot................................	21

Unit 1   Welcome!..22
♦ Vocabulary: School words • Numbers 11–20 • First, middle, and last names
♦ Language: Singular and plural
♦ Culture: Names in the US

Lesson 1	Marina at School...................................	24
Lesson 2	Filling Out a Form.................................	27
Unit 1 Project	Students in Your Class........................	31

Contents   **v**

Unit 2 Smile! 32
- Vocabulary: Family words • Numbers 21–30 • Telephone numbers • Addresses
- Language: *I you he she they*
- Culture: *Mr. Ms. Miss Mrs.* • *Excuse me. Please. Thank you. You're welcome.*

Lesson 1	Family Photos	34
Lesson 2	Your ID, Please	37
Unit 2 Project	Family Address Book	41

Unit 3 You're Sick. 42
- Vocabulary: Body parts and illnesses • Days of the week • Telling time • Numbers 40–50
- Language: *Is* with days, time, and health
- Culture: *Please repeat.* • Calling in sick.

Lesson 1	Your Daughter Is Sick	44
Lesson 2	Stay Home Today!	47
Unit 3 Project	Your Week	51

Unit 4 Money, Money, Money! 52
- Vocabulary: Money words • Numbers 60–100 • Months of the year • Dates • Places in the community
- Language: *Wh-* questions
- Culture: Cashing checks • Writing dates • Birthdays

Lesson 1	At the Bank	54
Lesson 2	Armando's First Paycheck	57
Unit 4 Project	Places You Pay Cash	61

Unit 5 No Milk 62
- Vocabulary: Names and types of food • *More* and *less, plus* and *minus*
- Language: *Need* and *like*
- Culture: Giving Change • Newspaper ads • Meals in the US • Men's and women's work • Pounds

Lesson 1	Grocery Shopping	64
Lesson 2	A Shopping List	67
Unit 5 Project	Going Shopping	71

Unit 6 Hurry Up! 72
- Vocabulary: Weather words • Transportation words • Clothing words • Places and signs in the community
- Language: *Do/don't Does/doesn't* • *Drive, ride,* and *take*
- Culture: *Nice day.*

Lesson 1	I'm Wet!	74
Lesson 2	I Need the Car	77
Unit 6 Project	A Class Map	81

Listening Scripts	82
Working with Maps	87
US Map	88
World Map	90
Alphabet	92
Numbers	93
Months, Days, and Time	94
Money	95
Topics	96
Language	97
Workbook Answer Key	98

Scope and Sequence

Unit Number and Title	Global Unit Theme (across all levels)	Unit Topic/Skill	Lesson-Specific Life Skills	Vocabulary	Language
Warm-Up Unit A Cecile's Day	Not applicable	Uppercase letters and numbers 0–10	Reading and writing the alphabet Alphabetizing Counting to 10 Spelling and writing your name	Uppercase letters Numbers 0–10 (words and numerals)	Not applicable
Warm-Up Unit B Omar's Day	Not applicable	Lowercase letters and colors	Reading and writing the alphabet Alphabetizing Identifying and reading colors	Lowercase letters Colors	Not applicable
Unit 1 Welcome!	Life stages: personal growth and goal setting	Beginning to study English	Writing first, middle, and last names Understanding classroom words Filling out a form	School words Numbers 11–20 First, middle, and last names	Singular and plural
Unit 2 Smile!	Making connections	Maintaining family ties	Identifying family members Showing ID Writing address and phone number	Family words Numbers 21–30 Telephone numbers Addresses	*I, you, he, she, they*
Unit 3 You're Sick	Taking care of yourself	Dealing with an illness	Calling in when taking a sick day from work Telling time Making and using a calendar	Parts of the body Illnesses Days of the week Telling time Numbers 40–50	*Is* with days, time, and health

Culture	Tasks and Unit Project	EFF Skills (The basic communication skills—read with understanding, convey ideas in writing, speak so others can understand, listen actively, and observe critically—are taught in every unit.)	SCANS Skills (The basic skills of reading, writing, listening, and speaking are taught in every unit.)	Technology
Not applicable	T1: Print name in uppercase letters T2: Count students (No unit project)	Not applicable	Problem solving	Not applicable
Not applicable	T1: Print name in upper- and lowercase letters T2: Ask and answer color questions (No unit project)	Not applicable	Interpret and communicate information	Not applicable
Names	T1: Copy classroom words T2: Write names in upper- and lowercase letters UP: Make a class name chart	Take responsibility for learning Cooperate with others	Organize and maintain information Problem solving Responsibility	Type classmates' names on the computer
Mr., Ms., Miss, Mrs. Polite words and phrases Male/female symbols Phone numbers and area codes	T1: Write about your family T2: Write a story about yourself UP: Make a family address book	Plan	Participate as a member of a team Organize and maintain information Understand systems	Type your family address book on the computer
The phrase *Please repeat* Calling in sick	T1: Complete a simple form T2: Write days and mark school days on a calendar UP: Make a calendar of your week*	Solve problems and make decisions Use information and communications technology	Understand systems Responsibility	Use a calendar form on the computer. Type your week's activities in the calendar

*Opportunity for portfolio assessment, using Oral and Written Rubrics

Scope and Sequence

Unit Number and Title	Global Unit Theme (across all levels)	Unit Topic/Skill	Lesson-Specific Life Skills	Vocabulary	Language
Unit 4 Money, Money, Money!	Personal finance	Identifying and using money	Writing dates Writing numbers and money amounts Doing basic addition Giving change Cashing a check	Money words Numbers 60–100 Months of the year Dates Places in the community	*Wh-* questions
Unit 5 No Milk	Consumer awareness	Grocery shopping	Writing a shopping list Doing basic addition and subtraction Checking the newspaper for prices of groceries Listing and writing information	Names and types of food *More* and *less* *Plus* and *minus*	*Need* *Like*
Unit 6 Hurry Up!	Participating in your new country and community	Getting to school and work	Talking about the weather Talking about transportation Using clothing words Recognizing places and signs in the community	Weather words Transportation words Clothing words Places and signs in the community	*Do/don't* *Does/doesn't* *Drive, ride, take*

Culture	Tasks and Unit Project	EFF Skills (The basic communication skills—read with understanding, convey ideas in writing, speak so others can understand, listen actively, and observe critically—are taught in every unit.)	SCANS Skills (The basic skills of reading, writing, listening, and speaking are taught in every unit.)	Technology
Cashing checks Writing dates Birthdays	T1: Count money and write amounts in numbers and words T2: Write places where you pay cash UP: Write a group and a class list of places where you pay cash	Use math to solve problems and communicate	Manage money Understand systems Arithmetic Decision-making	Use a calculator to add, subtract, multiply, and divide numbers.
Giving change Newspaper ads Meals Men's and women's work *Pounds*	T1: Write the store, street, and town where you shop for food T2: Write what you need from the store UP: Find out, write, and tell the class the name of a supermarket and the prices of foods, then answer class questions	Learn through research Reflect and evaluate Cooperate with others	Manage material and facility resources Participate as a member of a team Organize and maintain information Arithmetic Problem solving	Use a calculator to add prices of foods from the Unit Project
The expression *Nice day*	T1: Listen to the weather report; write about it or draw pictures T2: Draw a map of your community UP: Make a class map of your community showing class names and addresses*	Plan Cooperate with others Solve problems and make decisions	Understand systems Participate as a member of a team Problem solving Reasoning	Type a class list of names, phone numbers, and addresses

*Opportunity for portfolio assessment, using Oral and Written Rubrics

About This Series

Meeting Adult Learners' Needs with *English—No Problem!*

English—No Problem! is a theme-based, performance-based series focused on developing critical thinking and cultural awareness and on building language and life skills. Designed for adult and young adult English language learners, the series addresses themes and issues meaningful to adults in the United States.

English—No Problem! is appropriate for and respectful of adult learners. These are some key features:
- interactive, communicative, participatory approach
- rich, authentic language
- problem-posing methodology
- project-based units and task-based lessons
- goal setting embedded in each unit and lesson
- units organized around themes of adult relevance
- contextualized, inductive grammar
- student materials designed to fit into lesson plans
- performance assessment, including tools for learner self-evaluation

Series Themes

Across the series, units have the following themes:
- Life Stages: Personal Growth and Goal Setting
- Making Connections
- Taking Care of Yourself
- Personal Finance
- Consumer Awareness
- Protecting Your Legal Rights
- Participating in Your New Country and Community
- Lifelong Learning
- Celebrating Success

At each level, these themes are narrowed to subthemes that are level-appropriate in content and language.

English—No Problem! Series Components

Five levels make up the series:
- literacy
- level 1 (low beginning)
- level 2 (high beginning)
- level 3 (low intermediate)
- level 4 (high intermediate)

The series includes the following components.

Student Book

A full-color student book is the core of each level of *English—No Problem!* Literacy skills, vocabulary, grammar, reading, writing, listening, speaking, and SCANS-type skills are taught and practiced.

Teacher's Edition

Each teacher's edition includes these tools:
- general suggestions for using the series
- scope and sequence charts for the level
- lesson-specific teacher notes with reduced student book pages
- complete scripts for all listening activities and Pronunciation Targets in the student book

Workbook

A workbook provides contextualized practice in the skills taught at each level. Activities relate to the student book stories. Workbook activities are especially useful for learners working individually.

 This icon in the teacher's edition indicates where workbook activities can be assigned.

Reproducible Masters

The reproducible masters include photocopiable materials for the level. Some masters are unit-specific, such as contextualized vocabulary and grammar activities, games, and activities focusing on higher-level thinking skills. Others are generic graphic organizers. Still other masters can be used by teachers, peers, and learners themselves to assess the work done in each unit.

Each masters book also includes scripts for all listening activities in the masters. (Note: These activities are *not* included on the *English—No Problem!* audio recordings.)

 This icon in the teacher's edition indicates where reproducible masters can be used.

Audio Recording

Available on CD and cassette, each level's audio component includes listening passages, listening activities, and Pronunciation Targets from the student book.

This icon in the student book and teacher's edition indicates that the audio recording includes material for that activity.

Lesson-Plan Builder

This free, web-based *Lesson-Plan Builder* allows teachers to create and save customized lesson plans, related graphic organizers, and selected assessment masters. Goals, vocabulary lists, and other elements are already in the template for each lesson. Teachers then add their own notes to customize their plans. They can also create original graphic organizers using generic templates.

When a lesson plan is finished, the customized materials can be printed and stored in PDF form.

 This icon in the teacher's edition refers teachers to the *Lesson-Plan Builder,* found at www.enp.newreaderspress.com.

Vocabulary Cards

For literacy, level 1, and level 2, all vocabulary from the Picture Dictionaries and Vocabulary boxes in the student books is also presented on reproducible flash cards. At the literacy level, the cards also include capital letters, lowercase letters, and numerals.

Placement Tool

The Placement Test student booklet includes items that measure exit skills for each level of the series so that learners can start work in the appropriate student book. The teacher's guide includes a listening script, as well as guidelines for administering the test to a group, for giving an optional oral test, and for interpreting scores.

Addressing the Standards

English—No Problem! has been correlated from the earliest stages of development with national standards for adult education and ESL, including the NRS (National Reporting System), EFF (Equipped for the Future), SCANS (Secretary's Commission on Achieving Necessary Skills), CASAS (Comprehensive Adult Student Assessment System) competencies, BEST (Basic English Skills Test), and SPLs (Student Performance Levels). The series also reflects state standards from New York, California, and Florida.

About the Student Books

Each unit in the student books includes a two-page unit opener followed by three lessons (two at the literacy level). A cumulative unit project concludes each unit. Every unit addresses all four language skills—listening, speaking, reading, and writing. Each lesson focuses on characters operating in one of the three EFF-defined adult roles—parent/family member at home, worker at school or work, or citizen/community member in the larger community.

Unit Opener Pages

Unit Goals The vocabulary, language, pronunciation, and culture goals set forth in the unit opener correlate to a variety of state and national standards.

Opening Question and Photo The opening question, photo, and caption introduce the unit protagonists and engage learners affectively in issues the unit explores.

Think and Talk This feature of levels 1–4 presents questions based on classic steps in problem-posing methodology, adjusted and simplified as needed.

What's Your Opinion? In levels 1–4, this deliberately controversial question often appears after Think and Talk or on the first page of a lesson. It is designed to encourage lively teacher-directed discussion, even among learners with limited vocabulary.

Picture Dictionary or Vocabulary Box This feature introduces important unit vocabulary and concepts.

Gather Your Thoughts In levels 1–4, this activity helps learners relate the unit theme to their own lives. They record their thoughts in a graphic organizer, following a model provided.

What's the Problem? This activity, which follows Gather Your Thoughts, encourages learners to practice another step in problem posing. They identify a possible problem and apply the issue to their own lives.

Setting Goals This feature of levels 1–4 is the first step of a unit's self-evaluation strand. Learners choose from a list of language and life goals and add their own goal to the list. The goals are related to the lesson activities and tasks and to the unit project. After completing a unit, learners revisit these goals in Check Your Progress, the last page of each workbook unit.

First Lesson Page

While the unit opener sets up an issue or problem, the lessons involve learners in seeking solutions while simultaneously developing language competencies.

Lesson Goals and EFF Role The lesson opener lists language, culture, and life-skill goals and identifies the EFF role depicted in that lesson.

Pre-Reading or Pre-Listening Question This question prepares learners to seek solutions to the issues presented in the reading or listening passage or lesson graphic that follows.

Reading or Listening Tip At levels 1–4, this feature presents comprehension and analysis strategies used by good listeners and readers.

Lesson Stimulus Each lesson starts with a reading passage (a picture story at the literacy level), a listening passage, or a lesson graphic. A photo on the page sets the situation for a listening passage. Each listening passage is included in the audio recording, and scripts are provided at the end of the student book and the teacher's edition. A lesson graphic may be a schedule, chart, diagram, graph, time line, or similar item. The questions that follow each lesson stimulus focus on comprehension and analysis.

Remaining Lesson Pages

Picture Dictionary, Vocabulary Box, and Idiom Watch These features present the active lesson vocabulary. At lower levels, pictures often help convey meaning. Vocabulary boxes for the literacy level also include letters and numbers. At levels 3 and 4, idioms are included in every unit.

Class, Group, or Partner Chat This interactive feature provides a model miniconversation. The model sets up a real-life exchange that encourages use of the lesson vocabulary and grammatical structures. Learners ask highly structured and controlled questions and record classmates' responses in a graphic organizer.

Grammar Talk At levels 1–4, the target grammatical structure is presented in several examples. Following the examples is a short explanation or question that guides learners to come up with a rule on their own. At the literacy level, language boxes highlight basic grammatical structures without formal teaching.

Pronunciation Target In this feature of levels 1–4, learners answer questions that lead them to discover pronunciation rules for themselves.

Chat Follow-Ups Learners use information they recorded during the Chat activity. They write patterned sentences, using lesson vocabulary and structures.

In the US This feature is a short cultural reading or brief explanation of some aspect of US culture.

Compare Cultures At levels 1–4, this follow-up to In the US asks learners to compare the custom or situation in the US to similar ones in their home countries.

Activities A, B, C, etc. These practice activities, most of them interactive, apply what has been learned in the lesson so far.

Lesson Tasks Each lesson concludes with a task that encourages learners to apply the skills taught and practiced earlier. Many tasks involve pair or group work, as well as follow-up presentations to the class.

Challenge Reading

At level 4, a two-page reading follows the lessons. This feature helps learners develop skills that prepare them for longer readings they will encounter in future study or higher-level jobs.

Unit Project

Each unit concludes with a final project in which learners apply all or many of the skills they acquired in the unit. The project consists of carefully structured and sequenced individual, pair, and group activities. These projects also help develop important higher-level skills such as planning, organizing, collaborating, and presenting.

Additional Features

The following minifeatures appear as needed at different levels:

One Step Up These extensions of an activity, task, or unit project allow learners to work at a slightly higher skill level. This feature is especially useful when classes include learners at multiple levels.

Attention Boxes These unlabeled boxes highlight words and structures that are not taught explicitly in the lesson, but that learners may need. Teachers are encouraged to point out these words and structures and to offer any explanations that learners require.

Remember? These boxes present, in abbreviated form, previously introduced vocabulary and language structures.

Writing Extension This feature encourages learners to do additional writing. It is usually a practical rather than an academic activity.

Technology Extra This extension gives learners guidelines for doing part of an activity, task, or project using such technology as computers, photocopiers, and audio and video recorders.

Assessment

Assessment is completely integrated into *English—No Problem!* This arrangement facilitates your evaluation of class progress and provides a systematic way to set up learner portfolios. The pieces used for assessment are listed below. You may use all of them or select those that suit your needs.

Check Your Progress

This self-check, found on the last page of each workbook unit, is tied to the goals learners set for themselves in the student book unit opener. Learners rate their progress in life and language skills.

Unit Checkup/Review

For each unit, the reproducible masters include a two-page Unit Checkup/Review. You can use this instrument before each unit as a pretest or after each unit to assess mastery. If it is used both before and after, the score differential indicates a learner's progress.

Rubrics for Oral and Written Communication

The reproducible masters include a general rubric for speaking and one for writing (Masters 7 and 8). You can use these forms to score and track learner performance on the unit tasks and projects. Copy the rubric for each learner, circle performance scores, and include the results in the learner's portfolio.

About the Literacy Level Student Book Units

The literacy level student book differs from upper level books in several key ways. Here, vocabulary acquisition and listening skills are the central focus. While some structures and forms are taught as purely lexical items, very little traditional grammar is introduced until level 1.

To address the needs of preliteracy learners whose native language is not written or has a non-Roman alphabet, the first two units of the student book are warm-up units that introduce the alphabet, numbers, and colors, all within the context of a simple photo-illustrated story.

Unit Opener Pages

At the literacy level, Units 1–6 are 10-page units. Each reflects a four-skills approach to literacy instruction, and each includes a two-page unit opener followed by two lessons. One lesson focuses on listening skills, and the other focuses on reading skills. A unit project page completes each unit.

Unit Goals The vocabulary, language, and culture goals set forth in the unit opener correlate to a variety of state and national standards.

Opening Question and Photo The question "What do you see?" below the photo, the speech or thought bubbles in the photo story, and the photo caption introduce the unit protagonist(s), engage learners, and build a vocabulary base.

Picture Dictionary or Vocabulary Learners are introduced to general words and concepts, providing them with a linguistic and conceptual platform to move into the reading and listening lessons that follow. Literacy activities provide practice in writing the vocabulary just presented.

Lesson Opener Pages

In the two lessons that follow the unit opener, learners are involved with the character(s) as they navigate the situation and/or seek simple solutions to their problems. The lessons open with either a listening passage or a picture story. New or difficult words are boxed to call attention to them. Some of these words appear again in the Picture Dictionary or Vocabulary box.

Listening Passage A photo of the situation described in the listening passage appears on the first page of each listening lesson.

Picture Story with Comprehension Questions Reading lessons open with a picture story that has speech and/or thought bubbles and usually fills four frames. These picture stories build reading skills, establish the relationship of print and graphic material, and build lower-level inference and analysis skills. Sometimes an Attention Box flags words that may need to be explained. Questions below the picture story check reading and vocabulary comprehension.

Remaining Lesson Pages

At literacy level, the placement of the other lesson components is less controlled than at higher levels. The following components may appear where they are needed:

Picture Dictionary or Vocabulary At literacy level, Picture Dictionaries list picturable vocabulary words with illustrations. Other vocabulary boxes list nonpicturable words, letters, or numbers in context with related words.

Language A language box sometimes highlights basic language structures that learners practice in the unit.

Class or Partner Chat This interactive component models how to ask questions and write simple answers. The model sets up a personalized, realistic linguistic exchange that encourages use of the vocabulary and/or structures used in the lesson.

Learners work with a partner or talk with other classmates. At literacy level, learners are not required to manipulate language structures; they simply follow the model and record classmates' one- or two-word responses in a chart. A Chat Follow-Up may use patterned sentences to reinforce the language structure practiced in the Chat.

In the US At literacy level, this lesson element appears frequently, since building basic cultural awareness is a key goal.

Activities Practice activities apply what has been learned in the lesson up to this point. Very simple dictations are a frequent activity type at this level. The third or fourth page of a reading lesson usually features a short reading supported by visuals and containing carefully controlled vocabulary. After they read, learners write answers to questions. Often the task that follows requires learners to personalize the situation by writing about themselves using the vocabulary they have learned.

Tasks Each lesson ends with a task that represents the culmination and application of the skills presented and practiced in the lesson. The tasks practice life skills used in the real world and often help learners to personalize lesson concepts by relating them to their own lives. Most tasks can be done as in-class simulations rather than real-world homework assignments.

Unit Project

Learners apply skills acquired in the unit in a cumulative unit project. Each project is carefully structured, and is divided into three stages: Get Ready, Do the Work, and Present Your Project. Planning, organizing, collaborating, and presenting are important higher-level skills consistently developed in the unit projects.

Teaching Effectively with *English—No Problem!* Literacy Level

The following general suggestions for using literacy level *English—No Problem!* can enhance your teaching.

Before beginning a unit, prepare yourself in this way:
- Read the entire set of unit notes.
- Gather the materials needed for the unit.
- Familiarize yourself with the student book and workbook pages.
- Prepare copies of masters needed for the unit.

Materials

The notes for each unit include a list of specific materials. These lists do not include the following, which are recommended for all or most units:

- large sheets of paper (butcher or flip-chart)
- magazines, newspapers, catalogs (to cut up)
- art supplies (scissors, glue, tape, colored pencils, markers, colored and plain paper, etc.)
- a "Treasure Chest" box or other container of prizes (new pencils, pens, erasers, rulers, stickers, hard candy, small candy bars, key chains, and things collected at conferences or found at dollar stores)

Grouping

Working in groups increases learner participation and builds teamwork skills important in the workplace.

Learners can be grouped randomly. Four or five on a team allows for a good level of participation. For increased individual accountability, assign roles to group members. These commonly include
- group leader, who directs the group's activities
- recorder, who writes group responses
- reporter, who reports the group's responses to the whole class
- timekeeper, who lets everyone know how much time is left for an activity

Groups and roles within groups can be changed as needed.

Talking about the Photos

Contextualized color photos are used as starting points for many unit activities. Talking about the photos with learners is a good way to assess prior knowledge and productive vocabulary. For every photo, follow one or more of these suggestions:

- Ask general questions about what learners see: Who are the people in the photo? What is their relationship? Where are they? What's happening? What do you think is going to happen next?
- Point to objects in the photos, introduce new vocabulary words, and have learners repeat vocabulary. As learners name items in the photo, write new vocabulary on the board or an overhead transparency. Point to each word and have learners point to the corresponding item in the photo.
- When you want to talk about a particular object in the photo, begin by saying, "Look at the picture" *or* "Look here." Use your finger, a pen, a pointer, or a lighted overhead projector pen to focus their attention on the object.
- Ask questions from this teacher's edition, or make up questions of your own. It is difficult for learners at this level to produce language freely. They need prompts such as questions to help them converse.

Reading Titles and Captions

Literacy learners especially benefit from paying attention to titles and captions: these create a context for the unit or lesson. Try these suggestions:
- Point to the title or caption and read the words aloud.
- Have learners repeat the words several times.
- Write the title or caption on the board or an overhead transparency.
- Point to the words and say them again.
- Point to the words as learners say them aloud.
- Relate the words to the photo, learners' lives, and your own life.

Listening Activities

One lesson in each student book unit is driven by a listening passage. A variety of activities in the student book, as well as suggestions in this teacher's edition, help learners develop their listening skills.

Ideally, you will have access to a cassette or CD player and will be able to use the *English—No Problem!* audio recording. The recording allows learners to hear a variety of native-speaker and non-native-speaker voices. For teachers who need or prefer to read the audio portions, scripts for listening passages and activities are printed on pages 82–85 of the student book. Complete scripts for the passages and for all student book listening activities are on pages 82–86 of this book.

For listening activities, use the following sequence:
1. Review and model the directions.
2. Play the audio or read the listening script as often as learners want.
3. Have learners exchange papers or books to correct their answers.
4. Have volunteers write answers on the board or an overhead transparency.

Listening and Reading Comprehension

After listening to the passage or reading the photo story together, have learners complete the comprehension activity that follows it. Follow these steps:
1. Read the directions aloud. Mime them or write a prompt on the board (e.g., a circle around a word if the directions say to circle).
2. Read the first question or sentence stem aloud. Encourage individual learners to answer.
3. Complete the exercise by one of these methods:
   - Continue the exercise as a teacher-directed exercise if the class finds it difficult.
   - Ask learners to work in pairs, taking turns reading the items aloud.
   - Have learners read silently if they are able to work independently.
4. Finally, if you have not completed the activity together, have learners read the questions or sentence stems aloud and answer together as a group.

Follow-Up Ask similar questions to be sure that learners comprehend the passage or picture story. This might include sentence completions as well as *either/or, yes/no,* and *wh-* questions.

Ask additional questions that connect the reading to learners' own lives. For example, in the Unit 3 reading passage, Dyna's daughter is sick. Ask parents in your class if their children are fine today or if they are sick. Do the parents go to school if a child is sick, or do they stay home with the child? Do they go to work if a child is sick? Do they call work? Who do they call?

Vocabulary Practice

The primary focus at the literacy level of *English—No Problem!* is on learning words, not mastering grammatical forms. Spend plenty of time on Picture Dictionaries and Vocabulary boxes. Here are some suggestions for activities that help develop vocabulary.

Using Vocabulary Cards Use the Vocabulary Card Masters and card stock to make flash cards for all Picture Dictionary and Vocabulary words. Sets of words and pictures can be used for activities like matching, alphabetizing, sorting, and categorizing.

Consider duplicating the Vocabulary Card Masters in different sizes to accommodate various activities, e.g., a set of larger, laminated cards for whole-group activities, or individual sets for each learner. If you have a class set of scissors, have learners cut out their own cards.

Give learners plastic self-closing bags to keep their cards in, or use a hole punch and have learners put the cards on key rings or binder rings in their notebooks.

Introducing Vocabulary These steps will help learners comprehend the words:
- Point to the words or pictures as you read them.
- Read the words in random order and have learners point to the words or the pictures.
- Say each word again and have learners repeat.
- Write the words on the board or an overhead transparency. Point to the letters and have learners spell the words aloud.

Reinforcing Vocabulary Reinforce new words with these activities:
- Hold up a picture. First ask *yes/no* questions (e.g., "Is this an apple? Is this an orange?"). Later ask, "What is this?"

- Hold up a word card. Say, "Read this card."
- Pass around the cards and have each learner ask the question "What is this?"

Reviewing Vocabulary Ask learners to quiz one another by asking questions similar to those above. Or have one learner read a word and a partner find the corresponding picture. Have one learner say a word and the other spell it. (See also the section on Total Physical Response on this page.)

Writing Activities

Always model what you want learners to do. Review classroom instructions such as *read, write, circle, copy, trace* before each assignment. Walk around the room and watch learners as they write to make sure they understand.

After learners complete each activity, have them exchange books or papers to correct each other's answers. Write the correct answers on the board and review them. Learners who easily finish the assignment can do the One Step Up activities.

Class and Partner Chats

Learners need to move away from the book at times and develop confidence in using new language forms in a natural setting. Class and Partner Chats allow learners to move around and talk with their peers.

Preparing for a Class Chat Follow these steps:
- Make one copy of the Customizable Graphic Organizer Master (chart) appropriate for the Chat.
- Fill in the headings as shown in the student book.
- Duplicate and distribute copies of the customized graphic organizer.

Facilitating Class Chats Follow these steps:
- Ask learners to open their books to the Class or Partner Chat.
- Point to the speech bubbles, read them aloud, and have learners listen and repeat.
- Have a learner ask you the question. Answer honestly rather than following the model in the book.
- Ask a learner the same question. Elicit a personal response.
- Finally, have learners circulate (or, for Partner Chats, have them work in pairs), ask one another the same question, and record the answers on their charts.

Debriefing Follow these steps:
- Draw a large chart on the board or an overhead transparency.
- Fill in the appropriate headings.
- Ask learners for the answers they have recorded. Have them read from their charts.
- Write the answers on the chart for the class.
- Draw conclusions (e.g., *Many learners need bread today. Most learners are married.*), or, whenever possible, tally the results.

Chat Follow-Ups As a follow-up to each Class Chat, ask learners to write a few sentences in their notebooks based on the information they collected. Follow these steps:
- Use a learner's Class Chat chart to generate an example of the sentences that learners should write in their notebooks.
- Write model sentences on the board (e.g., *Shari has an umbrella. Shari doesn't have a raincoat.*).
- Have learners write sentences about other learners in the class.
- Circulate to assist learners with their writing.

Tried-and-True Techniques and Games for Literacy Level Learners

Total Physical Response (TPR)

TPR is a method for teaching language based on the premise that if we physically act out what we are trying to learn we are more likely to remember it than if we only read or hear about it. To adapt TPR to developing literacy skills using *English—No Problem!* try the following procedure:
- When teaching Picture Dictionary or vocabulary words, identify words that can be acted out (e.g., *point, write, sign, walk,* etc.).
- Demonstrate each word by acting it out as you say it aloud.
- Have learners say the word as you act it out, then as they act it out.
- Use the Vocabulary Card Masters or write the words on flash cards. Show the cards to learners while saying the words. Ask learners to read each card and perform the action.
- Show the cards to learners first in order and then out of order while learners mime their meaning. Speaking is optional.
- Give learners vocabulary cards. As you act out each word, have learners hold up the corresponding card.
- Ask learners to copy the words from the flash cards.

Dialogues and Role-Plays

Short dialogues appear throughout the units. These simple exchanges help new learners master common language forms. Follow these steps:
- Model the entire dialogue as learners listen.

- Have learners listen and repeat. Then assign one learner a part to recite with you and model the dialogue.
- Have learners practice the dialogues in pairs.

Role-playing is an excellent way to reinforce speaking skills. Follow these steps:
- Describe the situation.
- Assign roles to specific learners.
- Have learners act out the dialogue.

Class Stories

Class stories establish and reinforce the connection between speaking, reading, and writing. In *English—No Problem!* lesson photos are the stimuli for class stories. Follow these steps for writing class stories with literacy learners.

1. Have learners look at the photo and answer questions about it. *Either/or* questions force learners to supply the correct answer. *Wh-* questions demand a higher level of language proficiency than choice questions. *Yes/No* questions are easy to ask and answer but do not supply the vocabulary needed for the story.

2. Use the vocabulary from the lesson to write a story. At the literacy level, write sentence stems—the beginnings of sentences—for learners to orally complete. For example, write "Today is _____." on the board. Have learners say *Friday* and write *Friday* on the line. Then read the sentence with the learners. As learners become more proficient, you can dispense with sentence stems and simply ask questions and write answers.

3. Read the story and ask learners if they are happy with it. Make any changes they request. Read the story several times. Then have learners read it aloud together several times.

4. Have learners copy the story. While they are writing, circulate to monitor their work. Correct spelling and punctuation as needed. Point to words or sentences and have learners say them aloud.

5. Number the sentences on the board. Call out a number at random and have learners read that sentence aloud.

6. Read the story aloud with errors and have learners correct you. For example, if the correct sentence is "Today is Friday," say, "Today is Tuesday." Learners say, "No." Then ask, "What day is it?" Learners answer, "Friday." Read the story aloud again.

7. The following are just a few ways to provide additional literacy skills practice. To keep learners engaged, vary the practice activities from lesson to lesson.

    - Type the story, duplicate it, and give it to learners at the beginning of the next class. Call out key vocabulary words and have learners circle the words they hear. Or write the story on the board and have learners go to the board and circle the words.
    - Write the story sentences on sentence strips. Cut each strip in half, distribute them, and have learners find the matching half.
    - Write each word of a sentence on a separate card and have learners put the cards in order. Or, for an interactive activity, have learners stand side-by-side to make the sentence.

Pair Dictations

In these activities, one learner dictates words or numbers to a partner who listens and writes. Learners may need to be reminded not to look at their partners' papers until the activity is being corrected. As learners work, circulate to monitor their activity.

Spelling Dictations

A good way to begin a class is to do a spelling dictation of the vocabulary from the previous class.
- Select five to seven words for the dictation.
- On the board, or on learners' papers, number the words. After each number, write a short horizontal line for each letter in the word (e.g., 1. __ __ __).
- Spell a word and have learners write it. Repeat the spelling as many times as necessary.
- Have learners exchange papers to correct each other's work.
- Review by saying a word and having learners spell it as you or a learner volunteer writes it on the board. Ask learners to read the words.

Bingo

Use the generic bingo card (Customizable Master 1 in the reproducible masters) to review vocabulary for a unit. Duplicate the master and distribute one copy to each learner. Write unit vocabulary words on the board or an overhead transparency. (You will need 25 words.) Ask learners to choose words randomly and write a word in each square. Circulate to be sure they understand that they should write the words in random order.

Give each learner a pile of markers—dried beans, paper clips, pennies, or small squares of card stock. Then call out the words in random order and have learners place a marker on the word if it appears on their bingo card. The first learner to mark a row of five words down, across, or diagonally calls "Bingo!" and wins. Ask winners to read out the words they have marked and tell you the meanings.

Once learners understand the game well, have learners take turns calling out the words.

Concentration

Make vocabulary cards for the unit vocabulary words with the definition on one card and the word on another. Model the steps below:

1. Keeping words and definitions separate, learners arrange the cards in rows, facedown on the table.
2. Taking turns, learners turn over one word card and one definition card.
3. If the cards do not match, the learner turns them facedown again in the same place. A learner who finds a matching pair keeps the cards.

When all cards are matched, the learner with the most matches wins.

Twenty Questions

Give one learner a word card and have the others ask *yes/no* questions about the word. As the cardholder answers the questions, the other learners try to guess the word on the card. If after 20 questions no one has guessed correctly, the cardholder reveals the word, and play begins again with another learner holding a second word card. An easier variation of this game focuses on a particular beginning letter. After giving a learner a card, tell the class which letter the word begins with. Then play the guessing game with 20 questions.

Warm-Up Unit A: Cecile's Day

Materials for the Unit
- Paper and card stock
- Vocabulary Card Masters for Unit A
- 26 file folders labeled with letters A–Z
- Pictures of parking lots (optional)
- Unit Masters 9–10

Cecile's Day

Follow these steps to discuss the unit title:
- Draw a large face on the board to represent yourself. Write your name above the drawing and say, "My name is ___."
- Point to the drawing and say, "This is me." Draw four pictures to represent your day. Talk about them and say, "This is my day."
- Have learners look at the woman in the photo. Say, "Her name is Cecile. We are going to talk about Cecile's day."

Photo

Follow the suggestions on p. 5 for talking about the photo.

Read aloud the question below the arrow and ask these *either/or* questions:
- Is this a man or a woman?
- Is her name Cecile or Linda?
- Is she in a school or a parking lot?
- Is she looking for a car or a bus?
- Is this a *B* or a *C?* Is this a *C* or a *D?* (Point to letters on the signs.)

Using the answers to the questions above, write a class story. Write the sentences below on the board, leaving a blank for each word the learners selected. Your story may look like this:

>This is a <u>woman</u>.
>Her name is <u>Cecile</u>.
>She is in a <u>parking lot</u>.
>She is looking for a <u>car</u>.

Read the story several times. Have learners copy it. The way they hold their pencils and their ease or frustration in copying will help you

decide which learners need the English Beginnings units.

Caption

Before you read the caption, do this activity:
- Write large capital letters *B* and *C* on card stock or paper.
- Show each item and ask questions such as "B or C?" and "C or B?"
- Point to the "Row D" sign in the photo and explain the word *row*.

10 Unit A

Lesson 1: In the Parking Lot

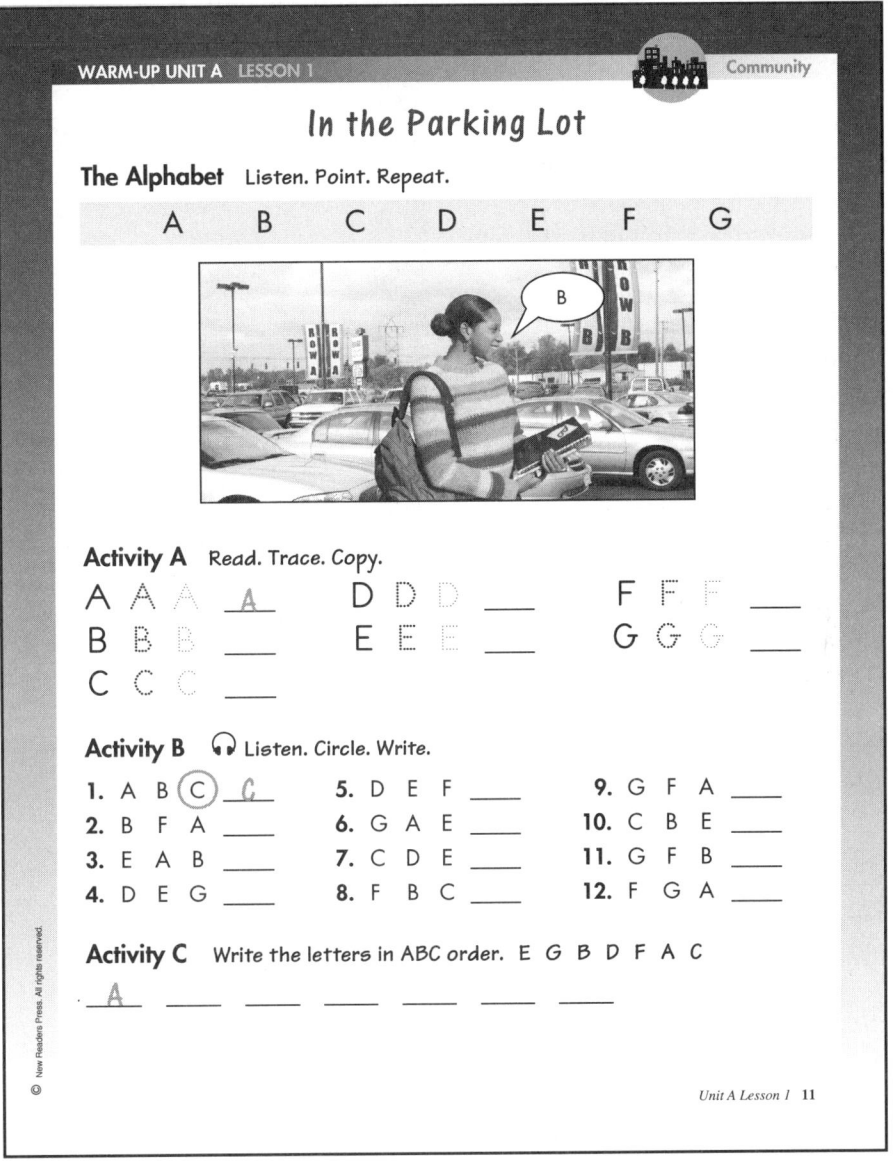

The Alphabet

Before learners open their books, do these things:
- Write capital letters *A* through *G* on the board or on large pieces of paper that you tape to the board.
- Say the names of the letters several times.
- Have learners repeat the name of each letter after you.
- Point to the letters randomly and have learners tell you the name of each.

Ask learners to open their books. Demonstrate the directions.
- Point to your ears and say, "Listen."
- Use your finger to point to the letter A and say, "Point to A." Repeat with all the letters.
- Have learners say each letter after you several times. Say, "A. Repeat: A."

Follow the suggestions on p. 6 for introducing vocabulary.

Follow the suggestions on p. 6 for making vocabulary cards. Use the Vocabulary Card Masters for capital letters.

Photo

Talk about the photo. Ask:
- Who is this? *(Cecile)*
- What is this? *(B)*
- Where is Cecile? *(in a parking lot)*

To establish the meaning of *parking lot*, show learners pictures of a variety of parking lots (supermarket, mall, etc.).

Activity A

Model the directions:
- Fold large sheets of paper in half.
- Draw dotted outlines of the letters *A* through *G* on one half of each piece of paper.
- With a marker, copy the same letters on the other half of the paper. Say *copy* each time you do this.

Make sure learners can see the direction of your pen strokes. Literacy learners often can copy letters, but their strokes may be incorrect.

Activity B

Play the audio or read the listening script below. Be sure learners know to go down the columns rather than across. You may need to demonstrate the activity, using an overhead transparency.

Listening Script/Answers

Listen. Circle. Write.
1. C   5. E   9. A
2. F   6. G   10. E
3. B   7. C   11. G
4. D   8. F   12. A

Activity C

Review the letters orally before learners write them in order.

Teach the first part of the alphabet song. Sing it at least five or six times.

Assign Workbook p. 4. Answers to workbook exercises are on pp. 98–100 of this Teacher's Edition.

Unit A Lesson 1 11

Lesson 2: At the Office

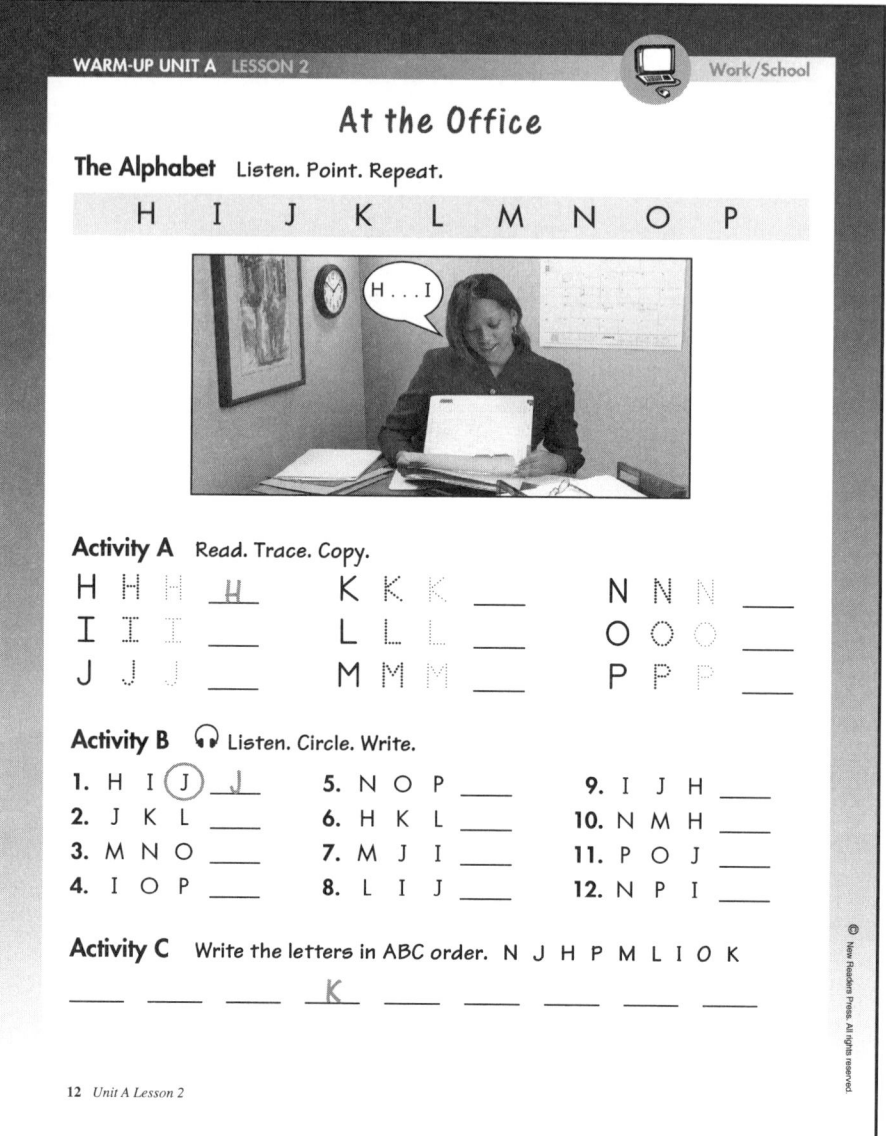

The Alphabet

Repeat the suggestions described on p. 11 for introducing letters.

Before you talk about the photo, hold up a file folder, say *folder*, and have learners repeat the word. Demonstrate how to put the folders in alphabetical order before you talk about the photo.

Photo

Ask these questions:
- Who is she?
- Where is she?
- What is she holding?
- What is she doing?

Extension

If possible, take learners to an office and have the staff show them the contents of file cabinets with alphabetized folders.

When you return to the classroom, put file folders labeled *H* through *P* in random order on a table. Arrange them in alphabetical order. Scramble them again, and ask for volunteers to put them in order.

Activity A

Follow the suggestions described on p. 11 for copying letters.

Activity B

 Follow the suggestions described on p. 11 for listening to letters.

Listening Script/Answers
Listen. Circle. Write.
1. J	5. P	9. I
2. K	6. H	10. M
3. N	7. J	11. O
4. I	8. L	12. N

Activity C

Follow the suggestions described on p. 11 for reviewing letters. Sing the alphabet song again, adding the letters *H* through *P*.

Snapping fingers, clapping, dancing, singing, etc., will help learners remember the names of the letters. To introduce the concept of order or sequence, try this activity:
- Draw three horizontal lines on the board. On the middle line, write *D*.

　　___　　_D_　　___

- Have learners give the names of the letters immediately before and after *D*.
- Do this for all letters *A* to *P*.

One Step Up

Have learners do an alphabet lineup.
- Give each learner a letter of the alphabet from *A* to *P*. If there are more than 16 learners in your class, repeat letters. Make sure to give out the letters in random order to make the lineup challenging.
- Have learners stand and put the letters in order.
- Repeat this activity each time you introduce more letters.

📖 Assign Workbook p. 5.

12 Unit A *Lesson 2*

Lesson 3 : At Home

The Alphabet
Follow the suggestions on p. 11 for introducing the letters.

Photo
Ask these questions as you point to people or things in the photo:
- Who is this?
- Where is she?
- What room is she in?
- What is she doing?
- Who is *she?* (Point to child in photo.)

Using the answers to the questions above, write a class story. Write the sentences below on the board, leaving a blank for each word the learners selected. Your story may look like this:
This is <u>Cecile</u>.
She is at <u>home</u>.
She is in the <u>kitchen</u>.
She is <u>cooking</u>.
This is her <u>child</u>.

Read the story several times with learners as you point to the words. To check learners' ability to distinguish letters, give them chalk or markers and have them come forward to circle the letter you say (e.g., if you say *S*, the learner should circle every *S* on the board).

Activity A
Follow the suggestions on p. 11 for copying letters.

Activity B
 Follow the suggestions on p. 11 for listening to letters.

Listening Script/Answers
Listen. Circle. Write.
1. S   5. Q   9. U
2. V   6. U   10. S
3. U   7. T   11. S
4. Q   8. R   12. V

Activity C
Follow the suggestions on p. 11 for reviewing letters and singing the alphabet song.

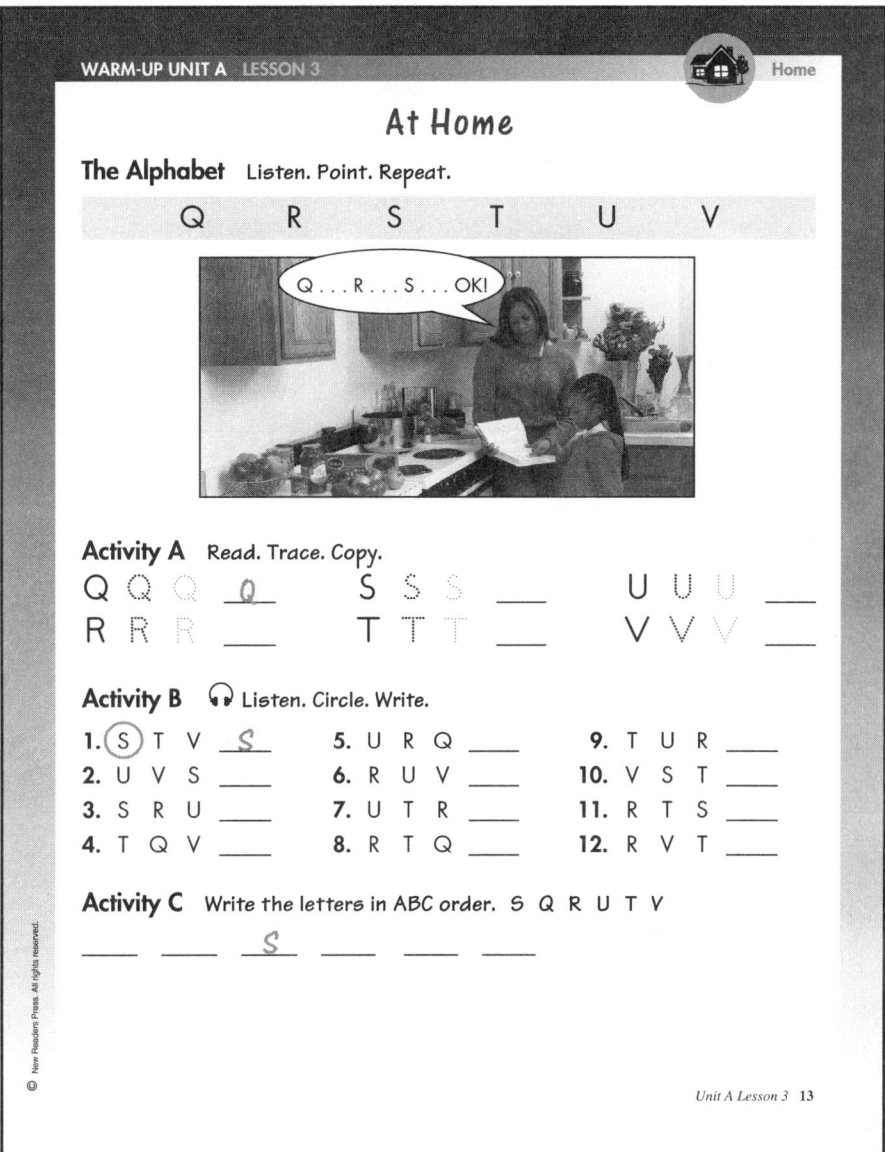

One Step Up
Draw a smiling face and a frowning face on the board. Write the word *spaghetti* on a piece of paper. Say, "I like spaghetti" or "I don't like spaghetti." Tape the piece of paper below the appropriate face. Then do a class survey. Write the number of learners who like spaghetti under the smiling face and the number who do not under the frowning face.

 Assign Workbook p. 6.

Unit A *Lesson 3* 13

Lesson 4: At the Pharmacy

The Alphabet
Follow the suggestions on p. 11 for introducing the letters.

Photo
Follow the suggestions on p. 5 for talking about the photo.

Follow the suggestions on p. 8 for writing class stories.

Activity A
Follow the suggestions on p. 11 for copying letters.

Activity B
 Follow the suggestions on p. 11 for listening to letters.

Listening Script/Answers
Listen. Circle. Write.
1. Y 4. X 7. Z
2. W 5. Z 8. Y
3. Z 6. X 9. W

Activity C
Follow the suggestions on p. 11 for reviewing letters and singing the alphabet song.

Extension
Model the following alphabet game before learners play.
- Select one learner (student 1) to say the alphabet to him- or herself.
- Select another learner (student 2) to say, "Stop," aloud while student 1 is saying the alphabet silently. Student 1 must then say aloud the letter she or he was saying silently when stopped.
- Student 3 must say words that begin with that letter (e.g., for v—*vegetable, video, VCR*).

Play this game periodically with other lessons. Often learners have larger speaking vocabularies than reading or writing vocabularies. You may be surprised at how many words your learners know!

Task 1
Have learners print their names and then spell them aloud. Next, have them line up according to the first letter of their first names. Then do another lineup by last names. If the class is too large for this exercise, have learners write their first and last names on pieces of paper or cards and work in groups to alphabetize them.

 Assign Workbook p. 7.

14 Unit A *Lesson 4*

Lesson 5: In the Parking Lot Again

Give each learner a vocabulary card with a number from 0 to 10.

Numbers
Follow the suggestions on p. 6 for introducing vocabulary.

Photo
Ask these *either/or* questions:
- Is this a man or a woman?
- Is she at home or in a parking lot?
- Is she looking for a car or a child?
- Is the license plate T32-879 or T-88-100?

Using the answers, write a class story:
This is <u>Cecile</u>.
She is in a <u>parking lot</u>.
She is looking for her <u>car</u>.
The license plate is <u>T-88-100</u>.

Activity A
 Play the audio or read the listening script below.

Listening Script/Answers
Listen. Write.
0, 1, 2, 3, 4, 5, 6, 7, 8, 9, 10

Activity B
 Play the audio or read the listening script below.

Listening Script/Answers
Listen. Circle. Write.
1. 2   5. 3   9. 4
2. 6   6. 7   10. 0
3. 8   7. 5   11. 9
4. 1   8. 10   12. 4

Activity C
Have learners write each missing number in order and say it.

Answers
1, 2, 4, 5, 7, 8, 10

Extension
Say *one,* and prompt a learner to say *two*. Continue until each learner has said several numbers.

Task 2
Divide learners into groups of no more than 10. Have each group count its members. Then have them count the women and men. Write on the board:
There are ___ students in my group.
There are ___ women in my group.
There are ___ men in my group.

 Assign Workbook p. 8.

 Use Unit Masters 9 (Reading: Letters and Numbers) and 10 (Game: Go Fish).

Unit Master 10
Give each learner a copy of Unit Master 10. Put learners in small groups. Have each group mix up their letter cards.
1. Have one person per group deal five cards to each player and place the rest facedown.
2. The learner to the dealer's left asks another player for a letter to match one in his hand. If the second player has any cards with that letter, she gives them to the asker.
3. The asking player places any pairs faceup and keeps asking for letters until he does not get one. Then he draws a card from the stack.
4. If he draws the letter requested, he shows it, lays down the pair, and asks again. If not, he keeps it, and play passes to the left.
5. Continue until a player has no cards left or the stack is gone. The most pairs wins.

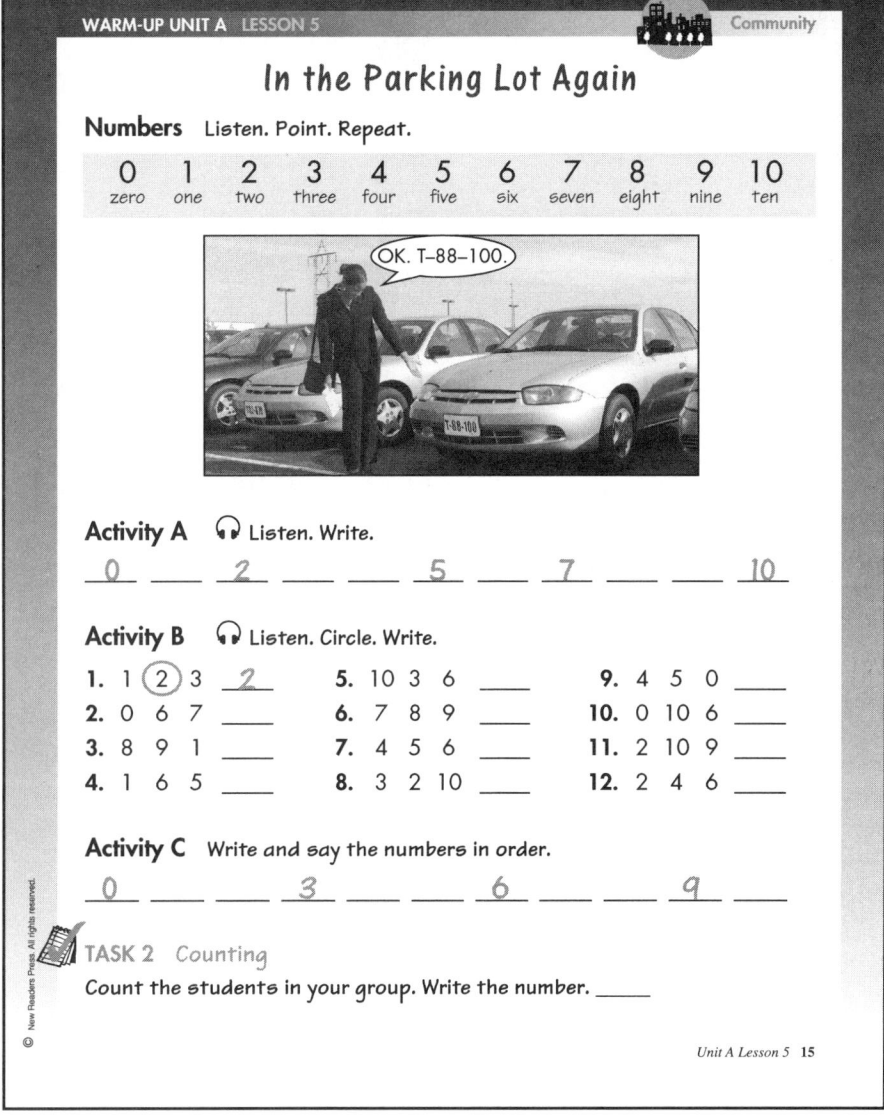

Unit A *Lesson 5* 15

Warm-Up Unit B: Omar's Day

Materials for the Unit
- Masking tape, card stock, index cards
- Small toy cars in a variety of colors
- Vocabulary Card Masters for Unit B
- Realia, photos, or drawings to establish the meanings of *at home, at school, bicycle, electric fan, teacher, student, book, office supply store, calendar*
- Prerecorded videocassette and DVD
- Game markers (paper clips, beans, plastic disks, etc.) and a coin
- Unit Masters 11–13
- Customizable Master 2

Omar's Day
Follow these steps to discuss the unit title:
- Write the words *Omar's Day* on the board.
- Point to the man in the photo and say, "This is Omar."
- Point to items and say the appropriate words.

Photo
Follow the suggestions on p. 5 for introducing the photo. Read the question below the arrow aloud and have learners tell you what they see. Write the words they say on the board. If learners have difficulty, ask these questions:
- Who is this?
- What is this?
- What color is this?

Using the words the learners have selected, write a class story. Your story may look like this:
This is Omar.
He is riding a bicycle.
He is on a busy street.
There is a _____ car.
There is a _____ truck.
There is a _____ bus.
The light is green.

Caption
- Before you read the caption under the photo, move a toy car along the top of a table and say *Go*.
- Then put three or four more cars in the path of the first car and ask *Go? How?*

16 Unit B

Lesson 1: At Home

The Alphabet

Before you focus learners' attention on the book page, do the following:
- Write capital letters *A* through *G* on the board.
- Review the names of the letters.
- Point to letters at random and have learners say the names.
- Write lowercase letters *a* to *g* under the capital letters.
- Point to lowercase letters at random and have learners say their names.

Follow the suggestions on p. 6 for introducing vocabulary.

Follow the suggestions on p. 6 for making vocabulary cards. Use the Vocabulary Card Masters for lowercase letters.

Photo

Follow the suggestions on p. 5 for talking about the photo.

Use photos or drawings to establish the meaning of *at home, at school, bicycle,* and *fan*.

Ask these *either/or* questions:
- Is this Cecile or Omar?
- Is he at home or at school?
- Is he in the living room or the kitchen?
- Is this a bicycle or a fan?

Activity A

Review the direction words *read, trace,* and *copy* by writing them on the board and modeling what learners should do. Monitor learners while they print the letters *a* through *g,* making sure they hold their pencils correctly. Have those who need more practice write the letters on lined notebook paper.

Activity B

 Play the audio or read the listening script below. Encourage learners to say "Please repeat" when they want to hear a letter again.

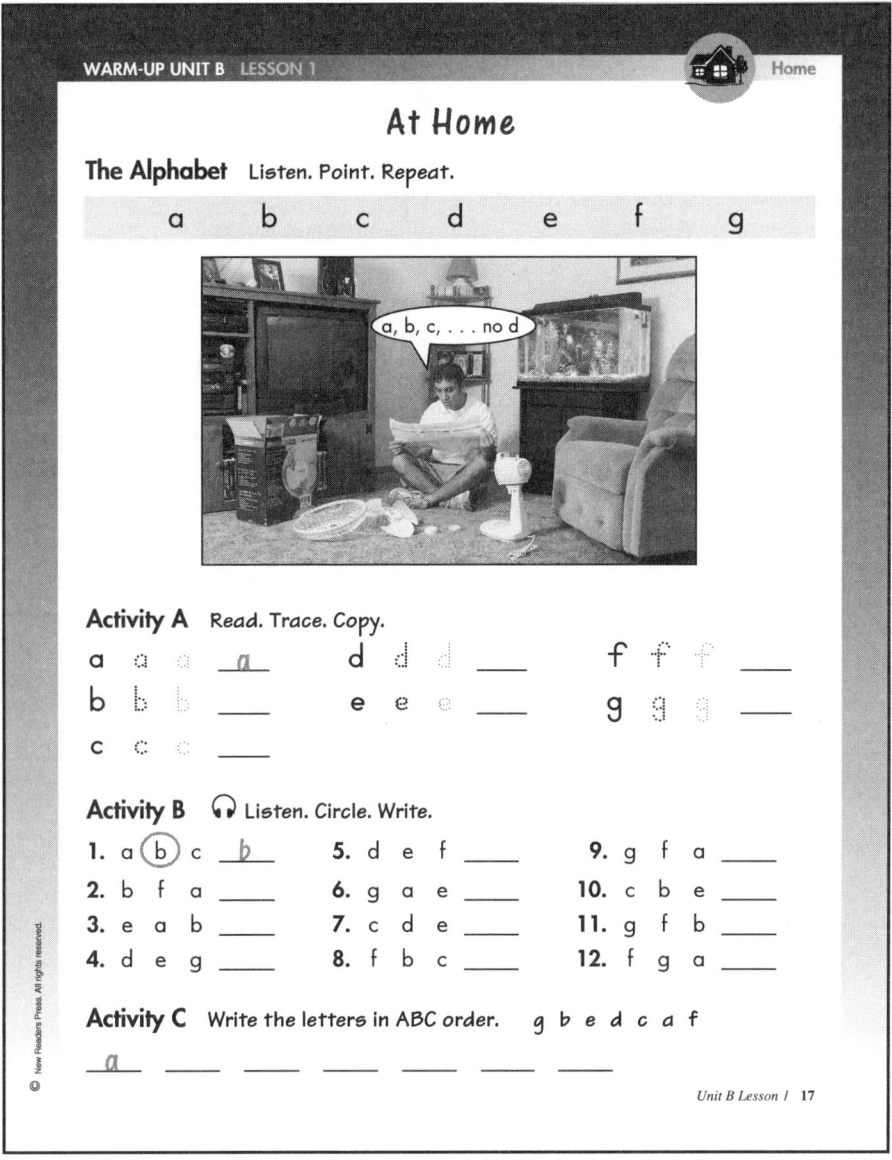

Listening Script/Answers
Listen. Circle. Write.
1. b   5. d   9. g
2. f   6. a   10. c
3. e   7. c   11. b
4. g   8. f   12. a

If learners need additional practice, do Activity B again, but dictate a different letter for each set. Have learners write these letters on a separate piece of paper.

Activity C

After learners have written alphabet letters *a* through *g* in order, write the letters on the board. Have learners say the names of the letters as you point to them.

Extension

Scramble the vocabulary cards for capital and lowercase letters, and give one card to each learner. Have learners walk around the room and find their match. Have the pairs line up in order and sing—one letter per pair—the alphabet song for *a* through *g*.

📖 Assign Workbook p. 9.

Unit B *Lesson 1* 17

Lesson 2: At School

The Alphabet
- Repeat the suggestions on p. 17 for reviewing the capital letters and introducing the lowercase letters.
- Use photos, drawings, or objects and people in your room to establish the meaning of *at school, teacher, student,* and *book.*

Photo
Ask these *either/or* questions:
- Is Omar at school or at home?
- Is he a teacher or a student?
- Is he writing or reading?
- Does he have a fan or a book?
- Does he say "h" or "j"?

Activity A
Follow the suggestions on p. 17 for reading, tracing, and copying letters.

Activity B
 Follow the suggestions on p. 17 for listening to letters.

Listening Script/Answers
Listen. Circle. Write.

1. h	5. n	9. i
2. k	6. l	10. m
3. o	7. j	11. o
4. p	8. k	12. i

Activity C
Follow the suggestions on p. 17 for writing and saying letters.

Sing the alphabet song again through the letter *p*. You can also sing the song, stop at a letter, have learners say it, and then continue the song.

Extension
Repeat the alphabet matching activity and lineup as described on p. 17.

 Assign Workbook p. 10.

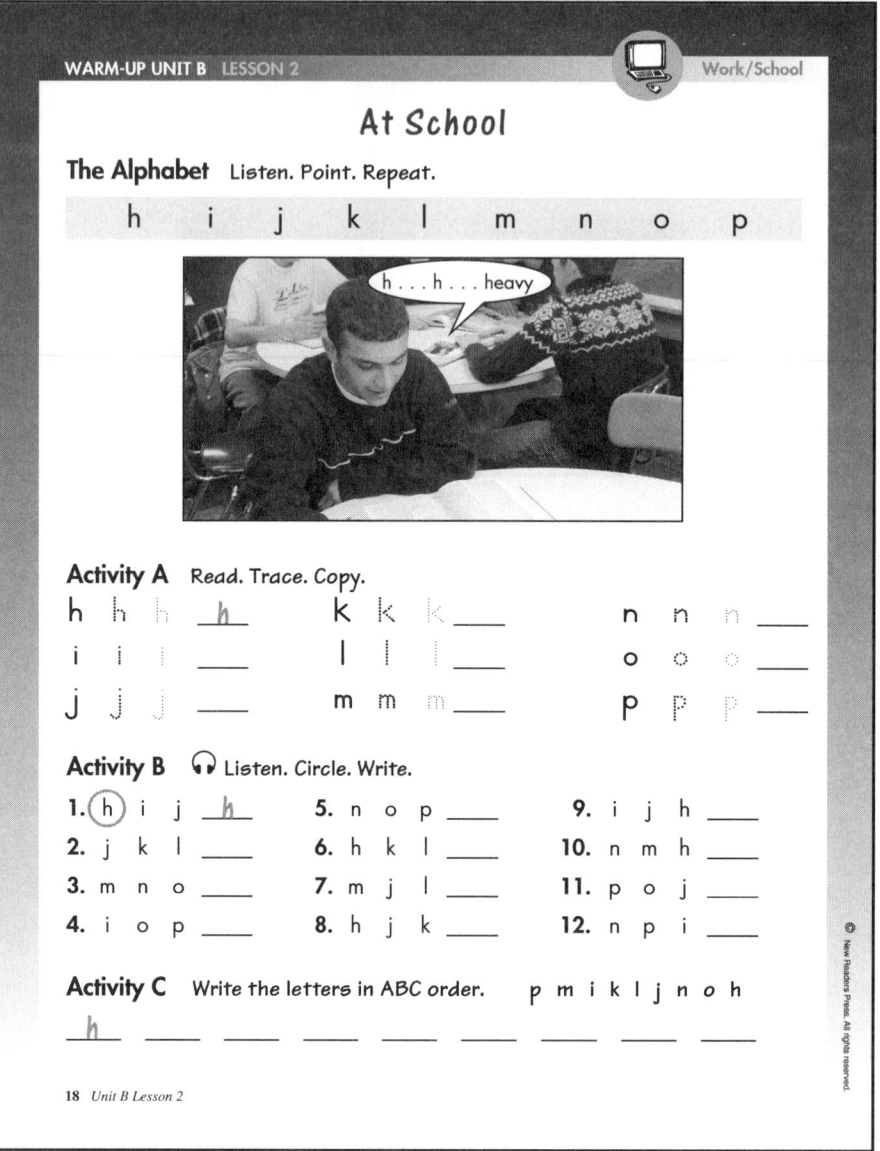

Lesson 3: At the Video Store

To introduce the lesson topic, do the following:
- Ask learners, "What's the number of this lesson?"
- Ask, "What's the title of the lesson?"
- Hold up a videocassette and ask, "What is this?" Do the same with a DVD.
- Do a survey to find out how many learners watch videocassettes and how many watch DVDs.
- Write sentences on the board using the responses:
  _____ students watch videocassettes.
  _____ students watch DVDs.
- Have learners copy the sentences.

Extension
Do a survey to find out where learners get their videocassettes or DVDs. Most libraries have videocassettes and DVDs for patrons to check out for free or at minimal cost. Find out from the local library what is available and share this information with learners.

Photo
Follow the suggestions on p. 5 for talking about the photo. Ask learners these questions:
- Who is this?
- Where is he?
- What does he want?
- What letter is he looking for?

Using the answers to the above questions, write a class story. Write the sentences below on the board and have learners tell you which words to write in the blanks. Your story may look like this:
  This is <u>Omar</u>.
  He is at a <u>video store</u>.
  He wants to rent <u>a videocassette</u>.
  He is looking for the letter <u>T</u>.

Read the story several times with learners as you point to the words.

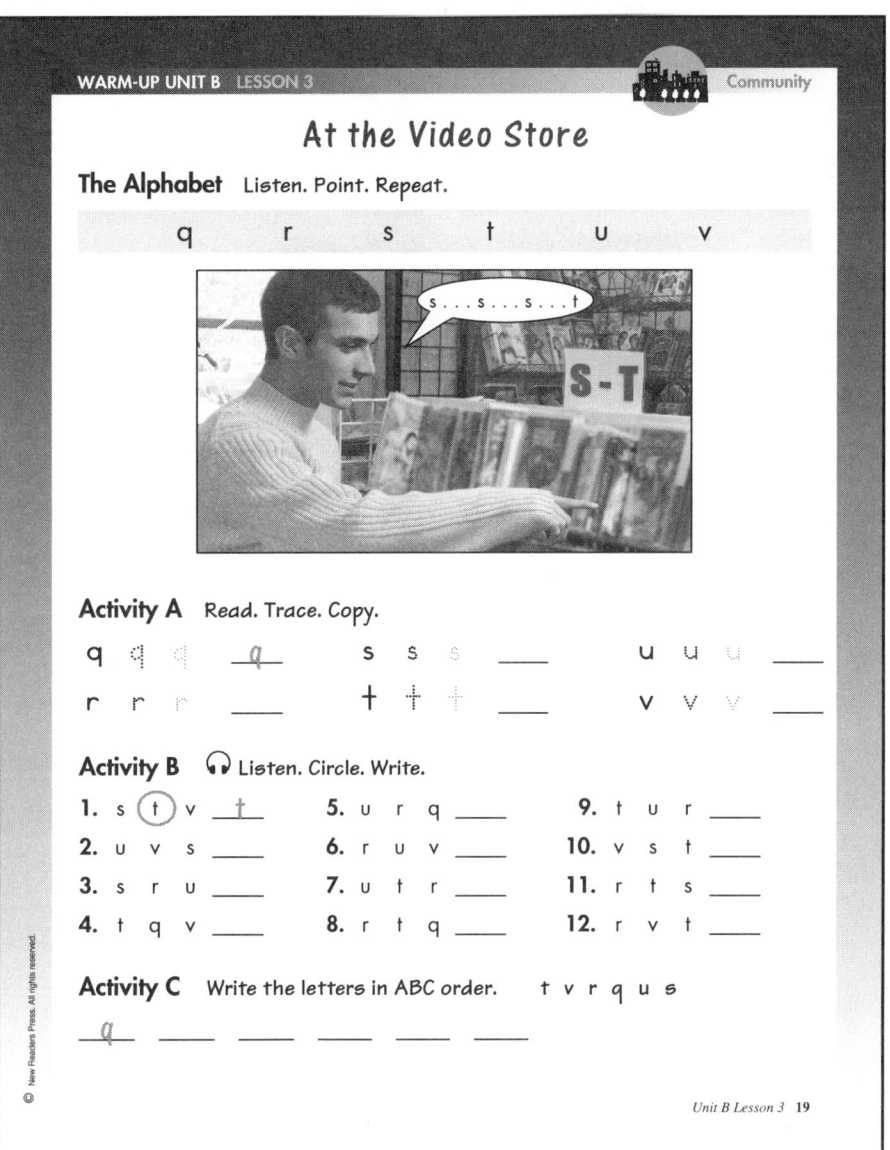

The Alphabet
Follow the suggestions on p. 17 for reviewing the capital letters *Q* through *V* and introducing the corresponding lowercase letters.

Activity A
Follow the suggestions on p. 17 for reading, tracing, and copying letters.

Activity B
 Follow the suggestions on p. 17 for listening to letters.

Listening Script/Answers
Listen. Circle. Write.
1. t   5. q   9. u
2. v   6. u   10. v
3. r   7. t   11. s
4. q   8. r   12. v

Activity C
Follow the suggestions on p. 17 for writing and saying letters.

 Assign Workbook p. 11.

Unit B *Lesson 3* 19

Lesson 4: In the Office Supply Store

Use photos or drawings to establish the meaning of *office supply store* and *calendar*.

The Alphabet
Follow the suggestions on p. 17 for introducing the letters *w* through *z*.

Photo
Follow the suggestions on p. 5 for talking about the photo. Ask these *either/or* questions:
- Is this Omar or Cecile?
- Is he at the video store or at the office supply store?
- Is he looking at an address book or a videocassette?
- Is he happy or sad?

Activity A
Follow the suggestions on p. 17 for reading, tracing, and copying letters.

Activity B
Play the audio or read the listening script below. Follow the suggestions on p. 17 for listening to letters.

Listening Script/Answers
Listen. Circle. Write.
1. y   4. z   7. x
2. z   5. w   8. y
3. w   6. x   9. z

Activity C
Follow suggestions on p. 17 for writing and saying letters. Sing the alphabet song.

Extensions
1. Prepare for this activity by writing the groups of letters introduced in each of the four lessons on large cards. Hang one card in each corner of the room.
   - Give each learner a letter of the alphabet. Ask learners to stand when you call out their letter.
   - When all learners are standing play a "Corners" game. Have learners walk around the room slowly as you say the letters of the alphabet. When you stop, learners must go quickly to the corner with their letter.
2. In a computer lab, call out letters, numbers, and names of colors and have learners type them.

Task 1
After learners complete Task 1, have them print their names on card stock. Check to make sure that the first letters of their first and last names are capitalized.
- Collect the cards, scramble them, and redistribute them.
- Have learners walk around the room saying their name to other learners until they find their name card.

Assign Workbook p. 12.

Extension
Use the Vocabulary Card Masters for capital and lowercase letters to play Concentration. (See p. 9 for how to play.) In this variation, a pair is a capital and a lowercase letter. Use half the letters (e.g., *A–M*) per game.

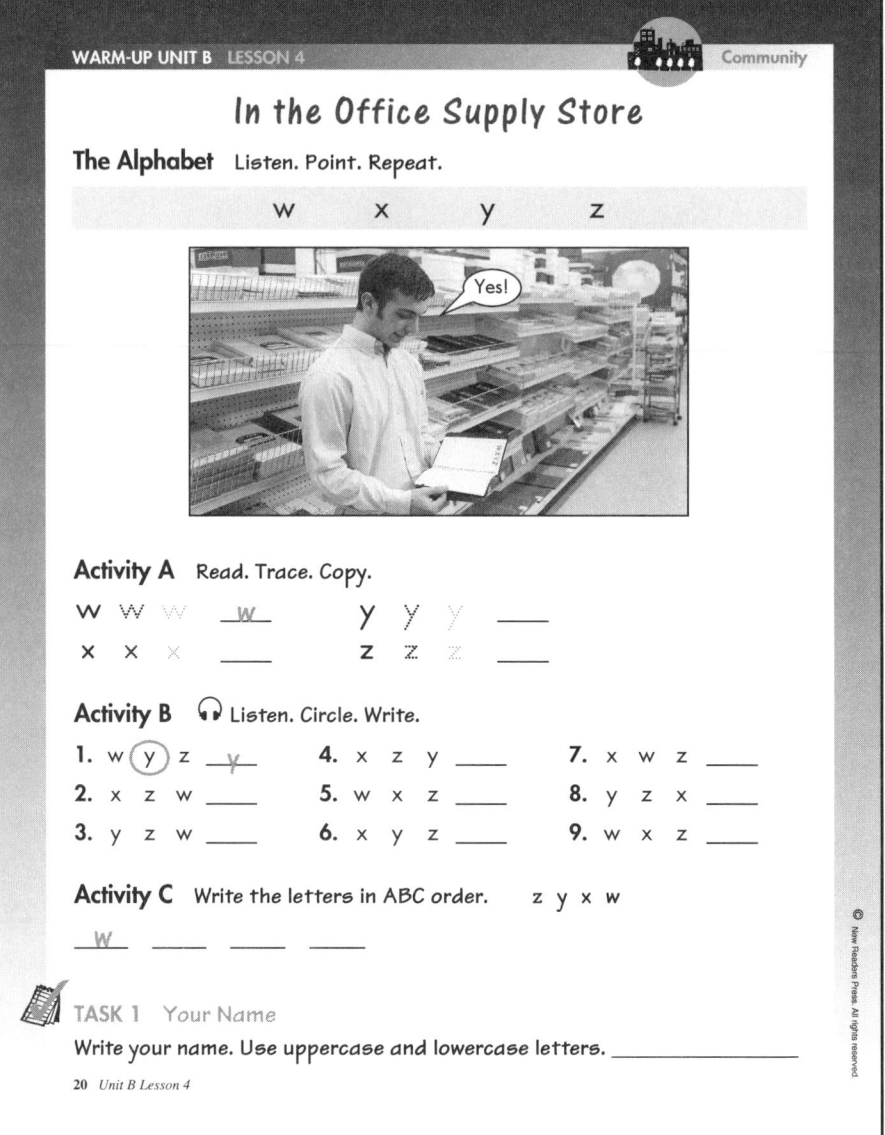

Lesson 5: At the Used Car Lot

Photo

Ask these *either/or* questions:
- Is this Omar or Cecile?
- Is this a bicycle or a car?
- Is it new or used?
- Is it blue or red?
- Are they at the office supply store or the used car lot?

Colors

Follow the suggestions on p. 6 for introducing vocabulary.

Follow the suggestions on p. 6 for making vocabulary cards. Use the Vocabulary Card Masters for colors.
- Make a set of nine cards showing the colors and nine showing the color names. If you have more than 18 learners, make duplicate cards. If you have fewer than 18, give some learners two cards.
- Say a color and have learners hold up appropriate cards.
- Tape the name cards to the board and have learners tape their color cards under the right names.

<u>Extension</u>
Point to objects in the classroom (books, notebooks, backpacks, etc.) and learners' clothing and ask, "What color is this?"

Task 2

Some learners may not have cars. If so, create cards for them with a color so they can participate.

Follow the suggestions on p. 7 for facilitating Class Chats.

<u>One Step Up</u>

 Use Customizable Master 2 (2-Column Chart). Make a copy and write the words *Name* and *Color* at the top. Then follow the suggestions on p. 7 (Preparing for a Class Chat) for duplicating the master and distributing copies. Have learners fill in the chart as they ask their classmates the question.

 Assign Workbook p. 13.

Use Unit Masters 11 (Reading: Find the Letter), 12 (Game: Going to School), and 13 (Game: What Color Is It?).

<u>Unit Master 12</u>
Give each group of three learners a copy of the game, a set of game markers, and a coin.
- Show them how to flip a coin and explain that each "head" allows them to move their markers one space, while each "tail" allows them to move two spaces.
- Have one learner in each group begin by flipping the coin and moving his or her marker. The learner must then say the word, letter, or number in the box on which the marker lands.
- If the player does not know the word, his or her turn ends, and play moves to the next learner.

<u>Unit Master 13</u>
Have learners work in pairs.
- Provide each pair with colored pencils or crayons and a copy of the master.
- Partner A reads each letter, number, and color name. Partner B colors the corresponding square on the grid.
- After they finish the first grid, they switch roles. Partner B reads, and Partner A colors.
- Tell learners what color to use for white.

 Assign Workbook p. 14: Check Your Progress.

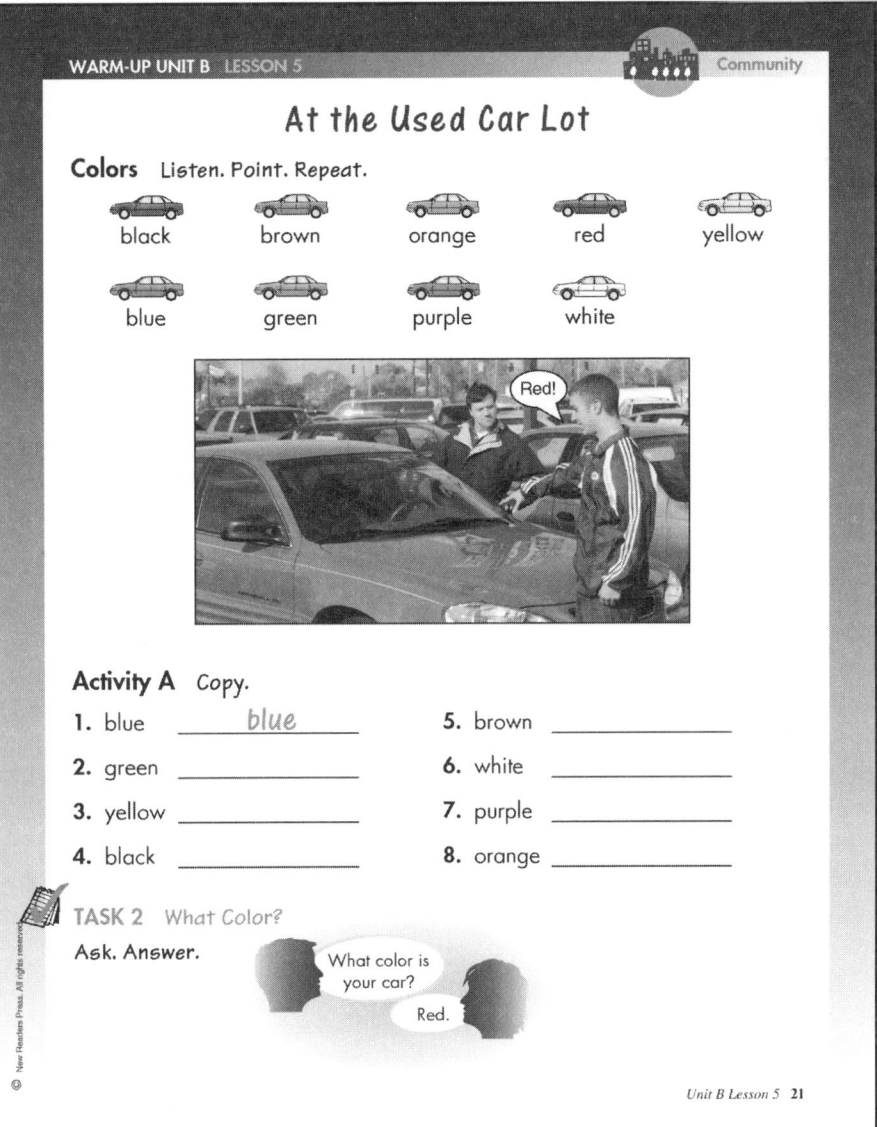

Unit 1: Welcome!

Materials
- Vocabulary Card Masters for Unit 1
- Vocabulary card for the letter *s*
- Sticky notes
- Common classroom items (see Picture Dictionary, p. 25)
- Registration forms
- Name tags
- Dice and paper clips, pennies, or other game markers
- Unit Masters 14–17
- Customizable Masters 1–3

Welcome!
Follow these steps to discuss the unit title:
- Write *Welcome* on the board in large letters.
- Ask a learner to leave the room and re-enter. Then, make a welcoming gesture with your arms and say, "Welcome!"
- Ask another learner to leave the room and re-enter. Repeat the welcome.
- Have learners repeat *welcome* after you several times.
- Call on individual learners and say, "Welcome."
- Ask another learner to leave the room and re-enter. Ask the class to say, "Welcome!"

Photo
Follow the suggestions on p. 5 for talking about the photo. Read the question below the arrow aloud. Many learners are familiar with the word *house,* but not *home.* Tell them, "My house is my home," and have them repeat the phrase after you. Then ask these questions:
- Is this a home or a school?
- Are there two people or three people?
- Is there one man?
- Are there two women?
- Are the people happy or sad? (Use facial expressions as you ask this question.)

Marina's Problem

Caption
- Read the caption aloud several times and have learners repeat it after you.
- Ask if the woman speaks English. Then ask if the young man speaks English. Have learners tell you what they think the unit will be about.

Picture Dictionary

Follow the suggestions on p. 6 for introducing vocabulary.

Follow the suggestions on p. 6 for using vocabulary cards. Use the Vocabulary Card Masters for the words in the Picture Dictionary.
- Show the cards to learners and say the words.
- Pass out the cards.
- Say a word and ask learners to hold up the correct card.
- Have learners repeat the words and hold up the corresponding card again.
- Have one learner say a word while the others hold up the corresponding card.
- Finally, mime the actions (listen, read, etc.) and have learners say the words.

Activities A and B

For each activity, circulate to check learners' work. Point to words randomly and ask learners to say them. Then point to words randomly and ask learners to spell them.

Activity B Answers
1. listen   5. classroom
2. write   6. office
3. speak   7. home
4. point   8. repeat

Extensions
1. Have learners work with a partner, using their vocabulary cards.
   - One learner shows a card. The other says the word.
   - To practice spelling, one partner can ask, "How do you spell _____?" The other partner spells the word.
   - Circulate to monitor the activity.
2. Give one learner an action-word vocabulary card.
   - Ask the learner to come forward and mime the action.
   - Repeat with other learners.

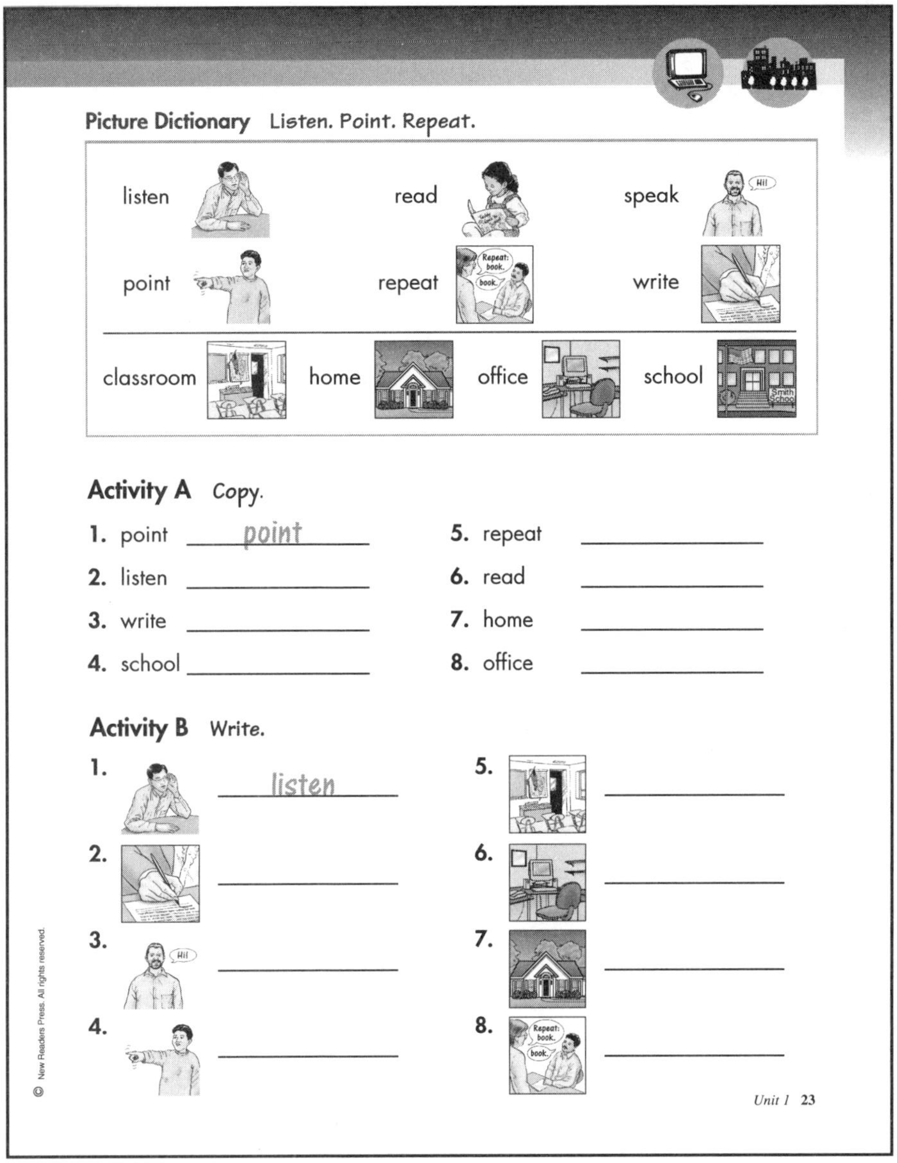

Use Customizable Master 1 (Bingo Chart). Duplicate the master and give one copy to each learner. Follow the suggestions on p. 8 for playing Vocabulary Bingo.

Unit 1 23

Lesson 1: Marina at School

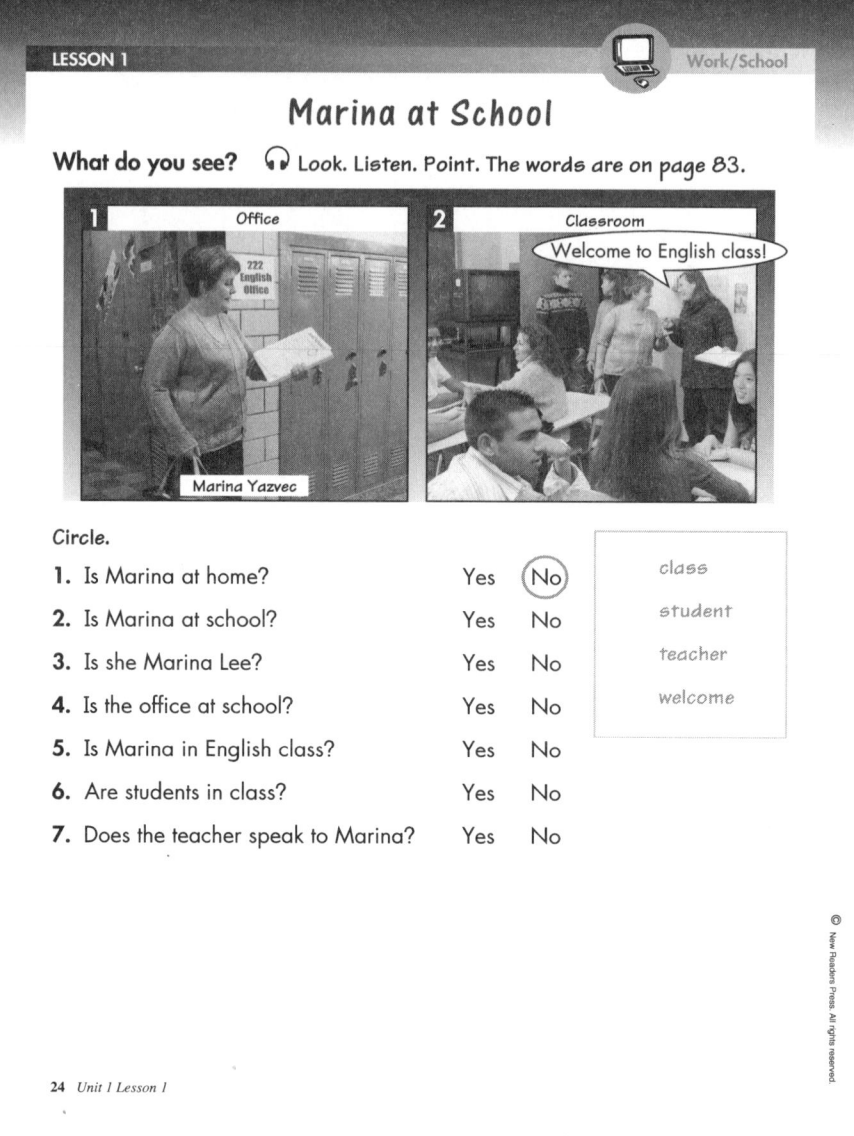

Photos
Ask learners these questions as you point to the photos:

Photo 1
- Is this an office or a home?

Photo 2
- Is this an office or a classroom?
- What class is it?

Read and point to the speech bubble, "Welcome to English class!"
- Mime the action by having a learner enter the room.
- Ask learners to listen and repeat the phrase.

Follow the suggestions on p. 5 for talking about photos.

Listening
 Play the audio or read the listening script below.

Listening Script
Listen.
One: Marina is in school. She's in the school office. Marina reads the classroom number.
Two: Marina is in the classroom. The teacher speaks to Marina. "Welcome to English class!"

Comprehension
Read the questions aloud and have learners circle the correct answer. Circulate to check their work. Listen as they answer *yes* or *no* to make sure that they understand the material.

Answers
1. No   5. Yes
2. Yes   6. Yes
3. No   7. Yes
4. Yes

Attention Box
Read the words to learners, pointing or miming to convey meaning. This vocabulary should be understood, but learners should not be expected to produce the words at this point.

24 Unit 1 *Lesson 1*

Picture Dictionary

Follow the suggestions on p. 6 for introducing vocabulary.

- Hold up the items and ask a series of *yes/no* questions. Example: Hold up a book and ask, "Is this a notebook? Is this a pen? Is this a book?"
- Vary the number of questions asked for each item. Sometimes the first question should be correct; sometimes four or five questions might be asked before learners can answer *yes*.

Follow the suggestions on p. 6 for using vocabulary cards. Use the Vocabulary Card Masters for the words in the Picture Dictionary.

Pass out vocabulary cards or sticky notes and have learners affix them to classroom items.

Activity A

Before learners do the activity, have them read and say the first set of words with you. Then play the audio or read the listening script. Have learners circle the word they hear.

Listening Script/Answers
Listen. Circle.

1. check   3. write   5. book
2. listen 4. pencil 6. speak

Activity B

Have learners read and then say with you the set of words in item 1. Then play the audio or read the listening script and have learners place a check mark in front of each word they hear.

Listening Script/Answers
Listen. Check.

1. teacher   3. circle
2. pen   4. student

 Assign Workbook pp. 15–17.

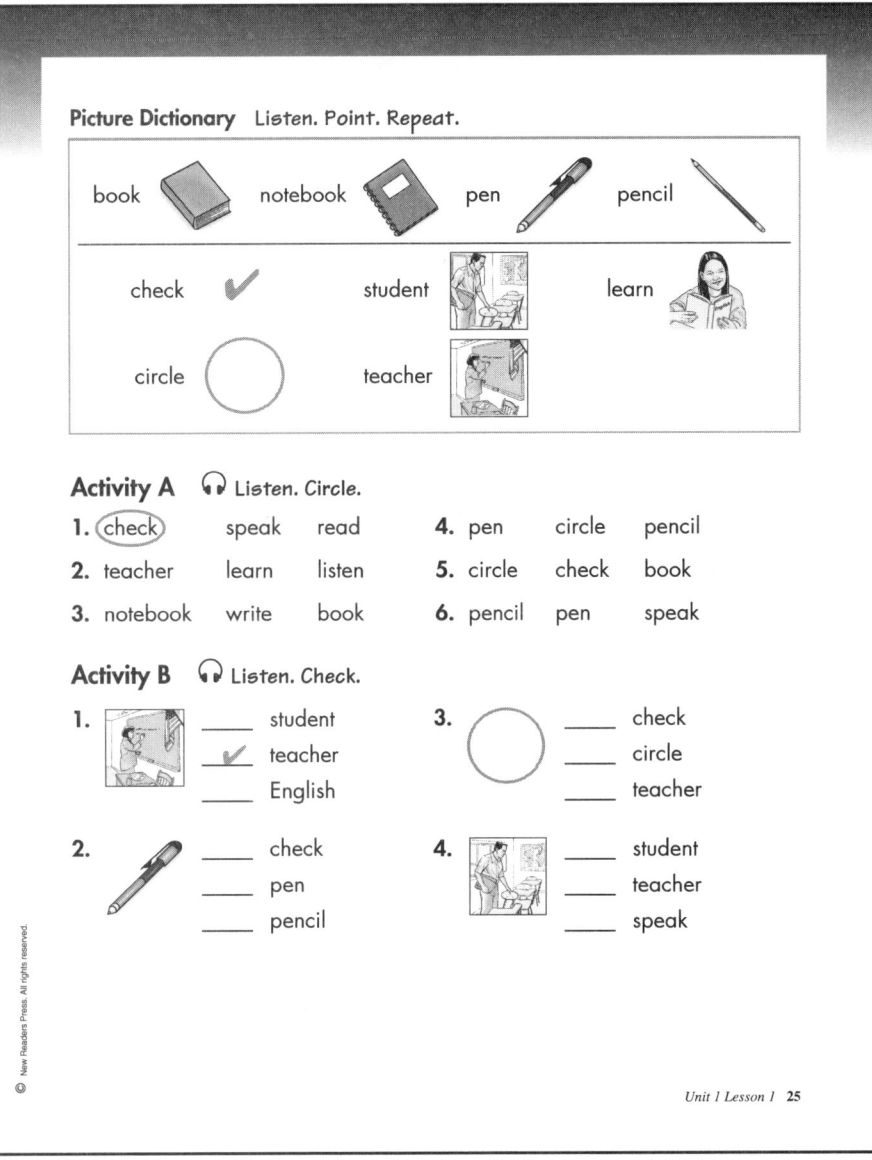

Unit 1 *Lesson 1* 25

Class Chat

Pass out name tags to all learners. Depending on learners' proficiency, you can write their names on the tags or have them write their own names.

- Use Customizable Master 3 (3-Column Chart). Make a copy of the master. Draw a line down the center of the second and third columns to make a five-column chart like the one in the student book. Then follow the suggestions on p. 7 (Preparing for a Class Chat) for customizing and duplicating the master and distributing the copies.
- Follow the suggestions on p. 7 for facilitating Class Chats.
- When learners have completed the Class Chat, do a class debriefing. Call out a name and ask the class to say the words or phrases that apply.

Class Chat Follow-Up

Use a learner's Class Chat chart to generate the sentences that learners should write in their notebooks. Write these sentences on the board or an overhead transparency. Circulate to help learners write sentences based on the chat.

Task 1

- Have learners walk around the classroom collecting words. Point out notices, signs, or other items on the walls where they can find new words to write in their notebooks.
- Encourage learners to read aloud the words they found.
- Write the words for them.
- Have them make corrections in their notebooks when necessary.

Extension

Have learners collect words from bulletin boards in the hallways and follow the steps above.

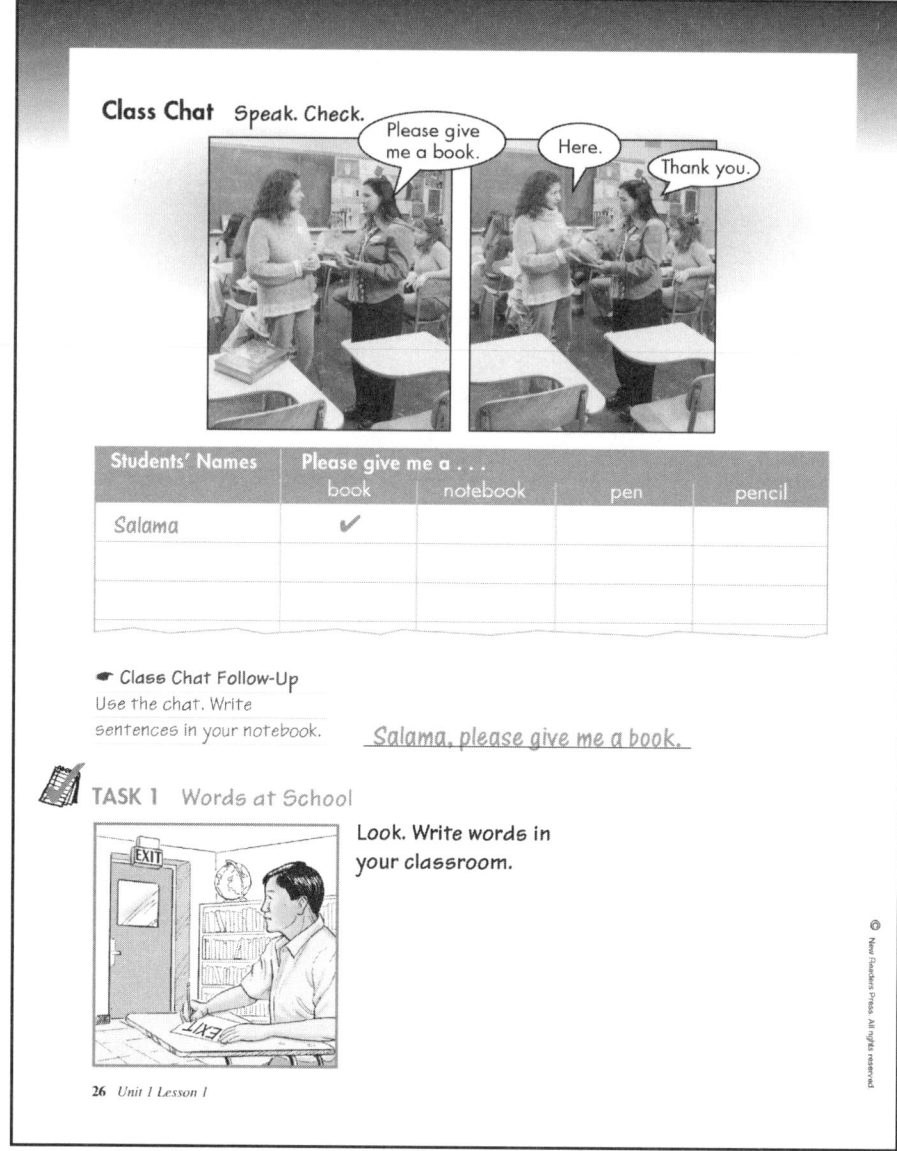

Use Unit Masters 14 (Reading: The Letter *P*) and 15 (Study Skills: Follow Directions) now or at any time during the rest of the unit.

Unit Master 15
- Prepare copies of the master for yourself and the learners. Number the words out of sequence on your copy.
- Lead the class in pointing to the words as you say them.
- Have learners write the numbers on the lines. Begin with the following prompt: "Number 1 is *check*. Point to the word *check*." The next one could be, "Number 2 is *read*. Point to the word *read*."
- The second time say, "Number 1 is *check*. Write the number 1 under *check*. Number 2 is *read*. Write the number 2 under *read*."

Lesson 2: Filling Out a Form

Photo

Read the lesson title and point to the form in the book. Follow the suggestions on p. 5 for talking about photos.

- Write your name on the board, spelling it aloud.
- Read the speech bubble, "Spell your last name." Ask a learner to spell his or her last name. Demonstrate with several learners. Have learners listen to the sentence again and repeat after you several times.

Ask these *either/or* questions about the photo:

- Where is Marina? Is she at school or at home? Is she in a classroom or an office?
- What is Marina doing? Is she speaking or writing? Is she listening or spelling?

Registration Form

Point to Marina's name on the form and spell it as you point to each letter.

Ask these *either/or* questions about the form:

- Is *Marina* her first or last name?
- Is *Anna* her first or middle name?
- Is *Yazvec* her middle or last name?
- Is the form for school or for work?

Comprehension

Ask learners to look at the three questions on the page. Read them together and have learners answer orally and then in writing.

Finish by asking a learner one of the questions and writing the answer on the board. Do this for all three questions.

<u>Answers</u>
1. Marina
2. Anna
3. Yazvec

Unit 1 Lesson 2 27

Picture Dictionary

Follow the suggestions on p. 6 for introducing vocabulary.

Demonstrate the concepts *first, middle,* and *last:*
- Have three learners line up one behind the other in front of the class. Point to the first, middle, and last person and say *first, middle, last.*
- Write your full name on the board. Under each name write *first, middle,* and *last.* Explain that *last name* means *family name.*
- Show how, in the US and some other cultures, people often use a single letter to represent a middle name. Rewrite your name using an initial for your middle name.
- Point out that each name begins with a capital letter. Underline each uppercase letter, pointing out its difference in height from the lowercase letters.

To provide additional practice, make cards of *first, middle,* and *last* for each learner.
- Have learners write the word *name* after each of these words on their cards.
- On the reverse side of the card, have them write their own names as they correspond to *first, middle,* and *last.* (Help learners who have difficulty determining which is a first or a last name.)
- Have learners put the cards in order, name side up. Ask them to walk around, look at classmates' cards, and read their first, middle, and last names.

Also demonstrate the word *form* with a registration form from your school.

Activity A

Read the entire dialogue twice. Then have learners listen and repeat.
- Ask learners to read the dialogue in pairs, taking turns doing each

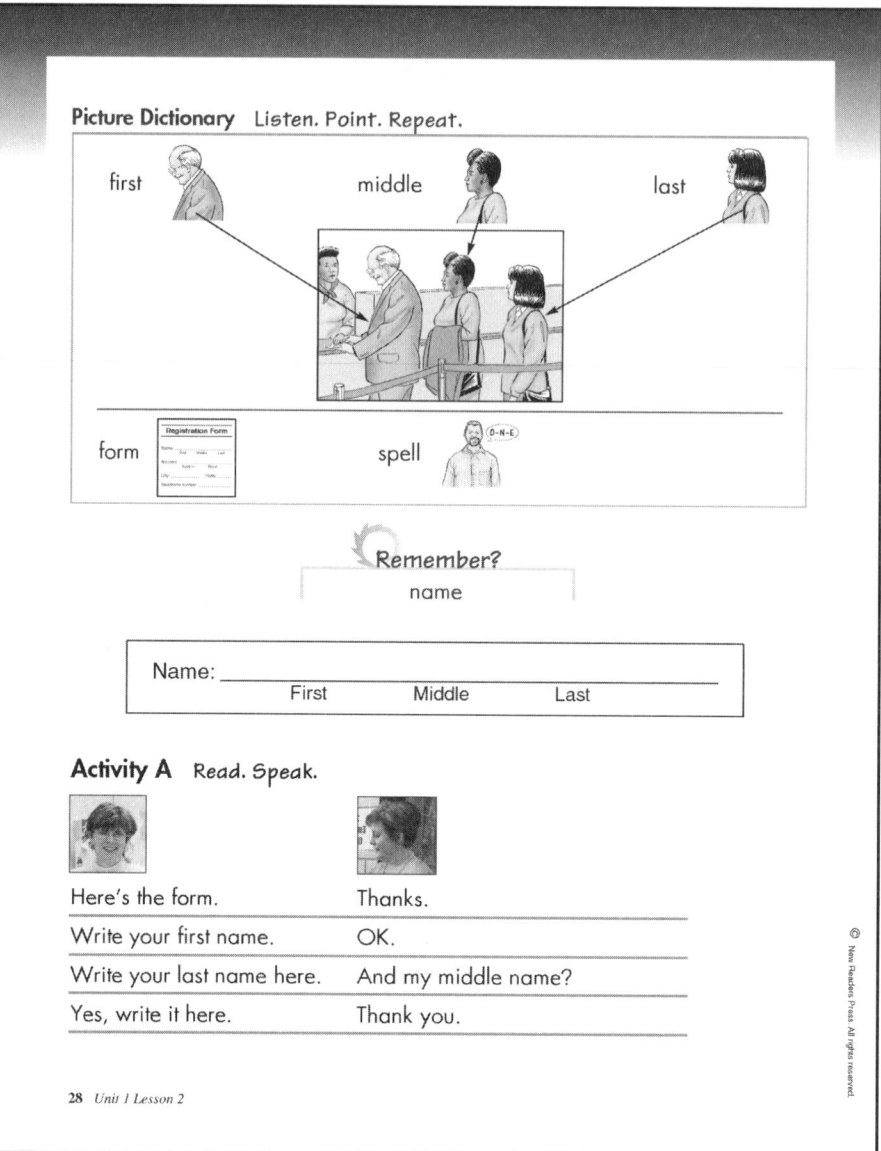

part. Circulate, listen, and offer assistance.
- Ask several pairs of learners to read the dialogue in front of the group.

Extension

Have a registration form ready so learners can role-play the dialogue between Marina and the school clerk. Ask one learner to leave the classroom and return as if walking into the school office. Ask another learner to play the role of the clerk. Have them perform the dialogue using the registration form.

One Step Up

Have more advanced learners ask and answer questions using personal information. Have other learners actually fill out as much as they can of the form.

Vocabulary

Follow the suggestions on p. 6 for introducing vocabulary.

Follow the suggestions on p. 6 for using vocabulary cards. Use the Vocabulary Card Masters for the words in the Vocabulary box.

- Read the numbers. Have learners hold up the vocabulary card for each number.
- Say the numbers randomly and have learners hold up the appropriate card for each.
- Have learners work with a partner and do the same thing.
- Have learners mix up their cards, exchange them with a partner, and put their partner's cards in order.

One Step Up

Have learners write the numerals 0 to 20 in their notebooks. Then have them write from memory the words for as many of the numbers as they can.

Language

Show the difference between singular and plural forms.

- Pass out a vocabulary card with the letter *s* to each learner.
- Demonstrate by saying a word and pointing to an item, first in the singular, then in the plural. Be sure to use only regular plurals. When you say a plural, hold up the *s*. Ask learners to do the same whenever they hear the *s*.
- Have learners listen, point, and repeat as you read. Then read the singular form followed by the plural, asking learners to repeat.
- Ask *either/or* questions using props (e.g., "Is this a book or are these books?"). Expect one-word answers—e.g., "book" or "books."
- Hold up or point to a book, pencil, notebook, or pen. Ask, "How many?" Have several of these objects ready so you can elicit different answers.

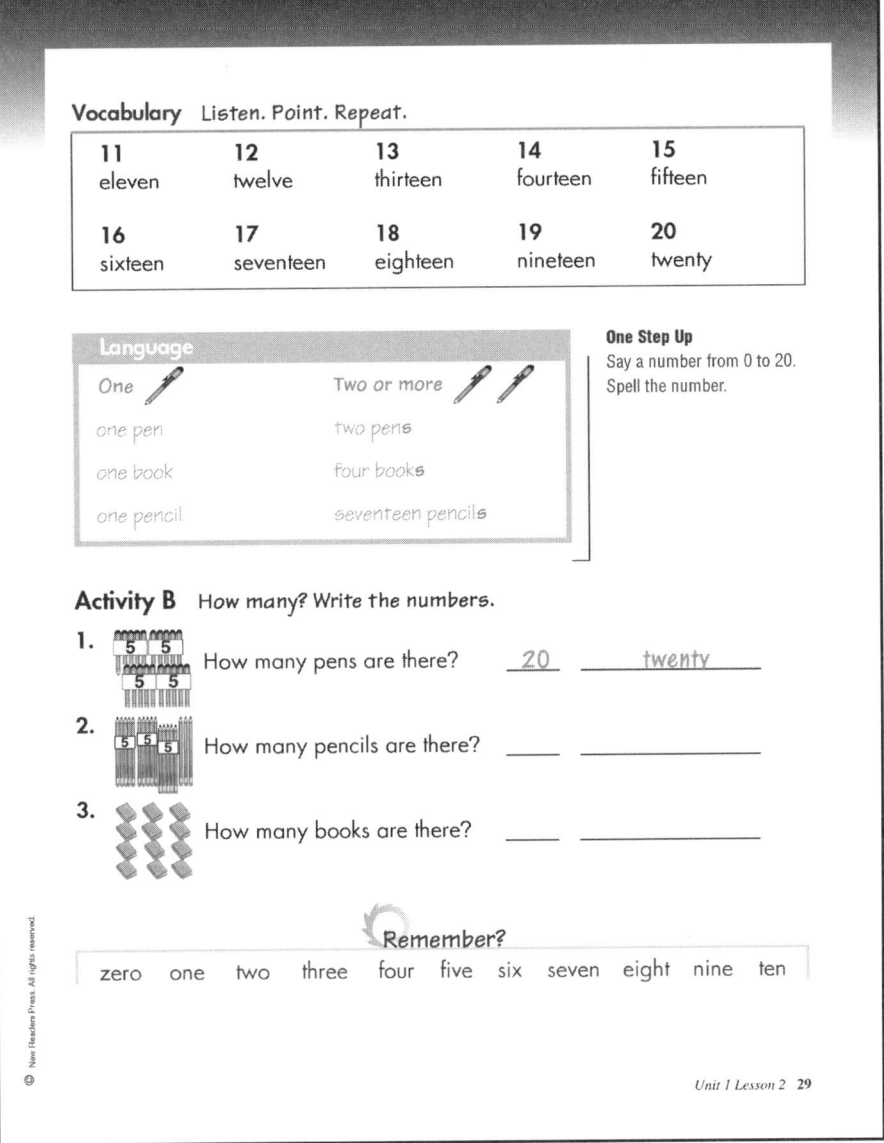

Activity B

Have students count the items in each picture and then fill in the blanks.

Answers
2. 18   3. 12

Assign Workbook pp. 18–20.

Use Unit Master 16 (Game: Is This My Classroom?) to practice the numbers 11 to 20.

- Duplicate enough copies of the master for learners to work in groups of three or four. On each copy, cut the doors of the classrooms so they open. On the inside of some of the doors write the name of a learner in that group.
- Pass out game markers and one die to each group. Model how to play, asking, "Is Room 15 my classroom?" Have learners repeat this question.
- Learners move around the board one die throw at a time. When they land in front of a classroom door, they ask the question, "Is Room ___ (the number on the door) my classroom?" Then they check by opening the door. When learners find their names, they are at their classroom. If not, play passes to the next learner. The first player to reach his or her classroom wins.

Unit 1 Lesson 2 29

In the US

- Using learners' name cards from the exercise on p. 28, demonstrate the difference between cultures by showing how someone's name is ordered in their home country. You can also use the example in the book—Ester Elena Gomez Sanchez.
- Point out that in Spanish-speaking countries, people use both their mother's and father's (or father's and husband's) last names. (You could point out that some women in the US do this today with a hyphenated last name.) In Asian countries, the family name usually comes first. Explain that in the US, the family name is last and people often use only one last name.
- Have learners repeat the question and answer in the speech bubbles.
- Have them ask one another, "How many names do you use in your country?"

Class Chat

 Use Customizable Master 2 (2-Column Chart).

- Make a copy of the master.
- Divide the columns in half, creating a four-column chart.
- Follow the model in the student book for writing the column heads.
- Make copies and distribute them to learners.

Follow the suggestions on p. 7 for facilitating Class Chats.

- Have learners ask four people to spell their names so they can enter them in their notebooks.
- Encourage learners to pronounce the names as they write them.

Class Chat Follow-Up

Have learners write the names from the chat in their notebooks.

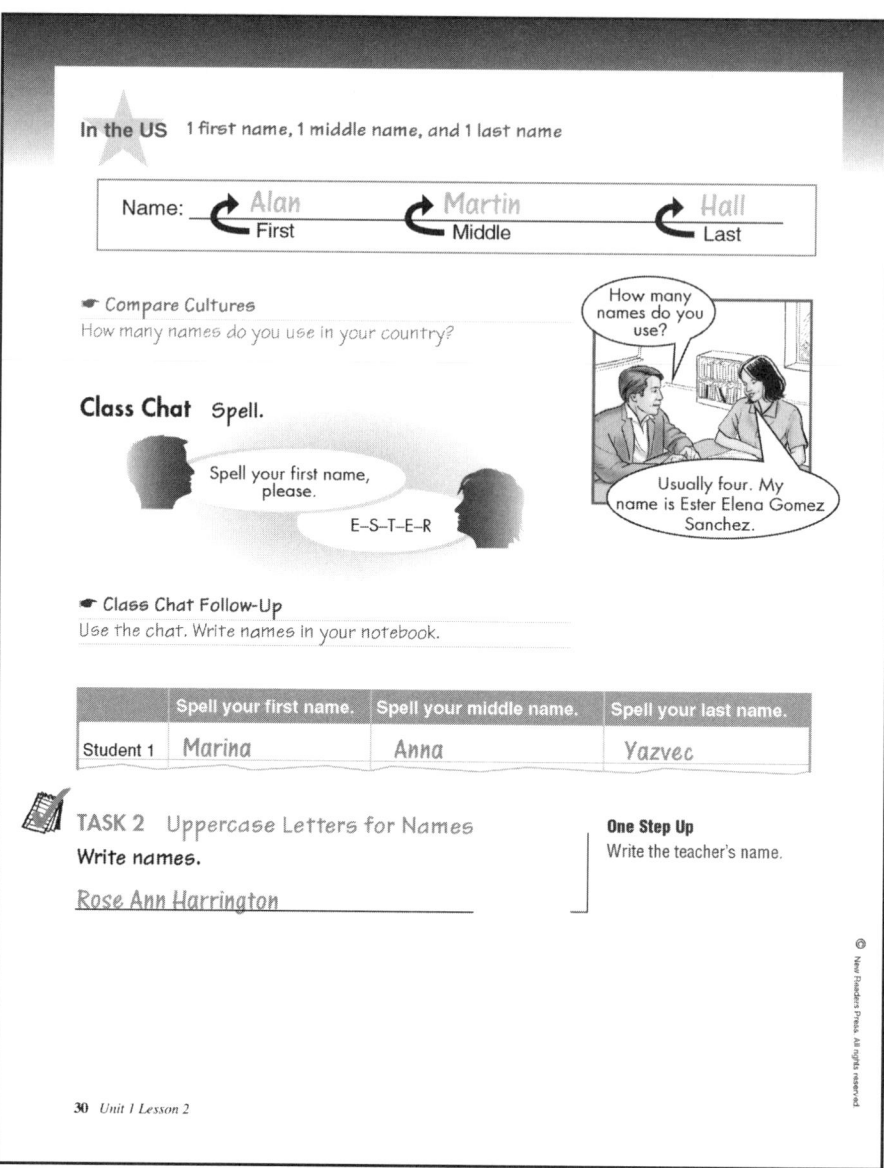

Task 2

Write your own name on the board, making sure to emphasize the capital letters.

- Have learners copy your name and the names of two or three learners from their Class Chat charts.
- Circulate to monitor their work to be sure they have written the capital letters correctly.

30 Unit 1 Lesson 2

Unit 1 Project

Each learner applies the vocabulary and concepts from the unit to create an alphabetized list of class names. Knowing their classmates' names is also a good way for learners to develop a sense of camaraderie in the classroom.

Get Ready

Duplicate and distribute Customizable Master 2 (2-Column Chart). Have two copies available for each learner.

Do the Work

Ask learners to write the names of everyone in the class.
- If you have an exceptionally large class, ask them to write only a limited number of names. Give learners ample time to complete this activity.
- When they finish, have them put the names in alphabetical order by last name. If this is too difficult for some to do alone, have learners work in pairs or groups.

Present Your Project

Ask learners to read their lists aloud to the class. For large classes, ask learners to read aloud just 10 names each.

Technology Extra

Set up a table or chart on the computer into which learners can type the names.

One Step Up

Show learners how to use the Shift key to produce a capital letter. Have them type at least some names on the list with the first letter capitalized. Make sure learners use the Shift key rather than the Caps Lock key.

Assign Workbook p. 21: Check Your Progress. Complete the first Progress Check as a class to show how it should be completed. Demonstrate how to write a check mark.

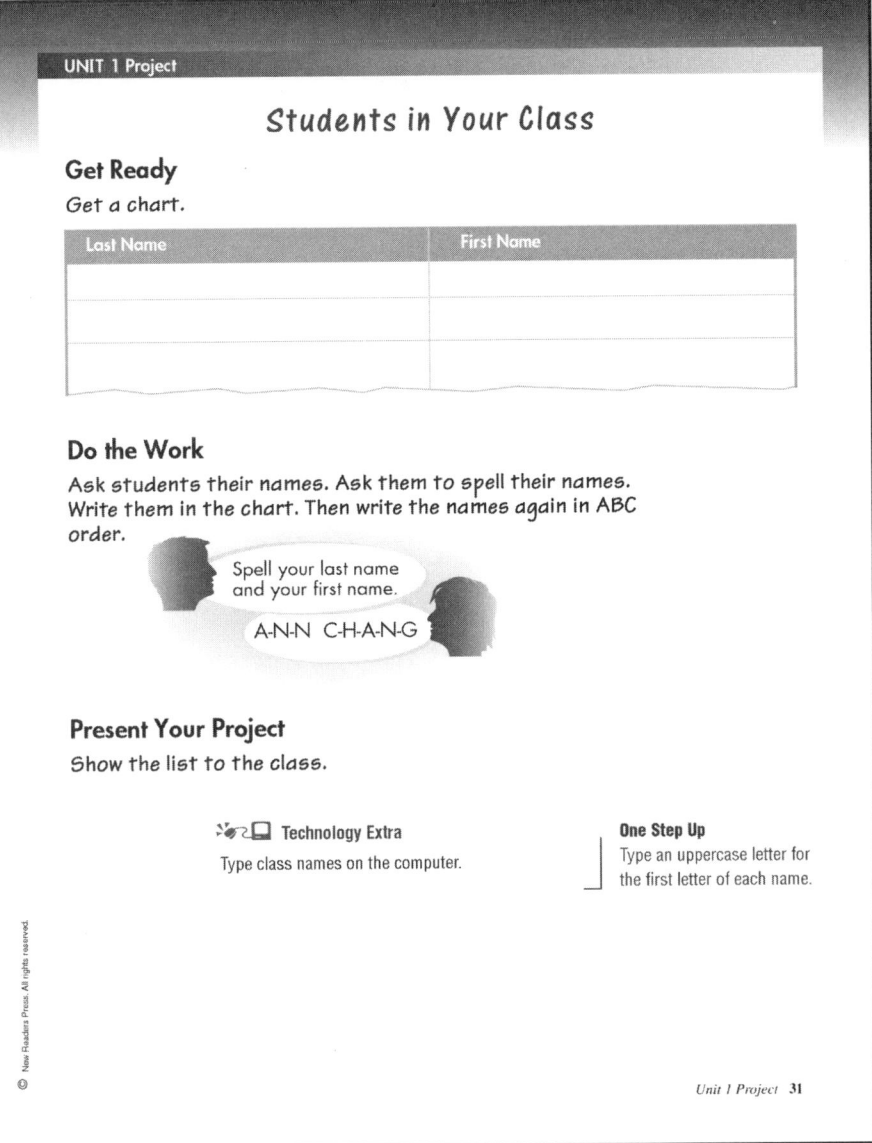

Use Unit Master 17 (Unit 1 Checkup/Review) to assess learner progress.

Unit 2: Smile!

Materials for the Unit
- Vocabulary Card Masters for Unit 2
- Pictures of restroom doors (optional)
- Camera
- Photos of your family
- Magazine pictures of people of different genders, ethnicities, and ages
- Photos of objects you like and dislike
- Index cards
- Coins and game markers
- Unit Masters 18–22
- Customizable Masters 1–3, 5

Smile!
Follow these steps to discuss the unit title:
- Draw a big smiling face on the board.
- Stand to the left of the face and make your face expressionless. Then stand to the right of the face and smile.
- Have learners say "Smile!" several times.
- Call on individual learners. Say "Smile!" and encourage them to smile.
- Have learners tell each other to smile.

Photo
Follow the suggestions on p. 5 for talking about the photo.
Read the question below the arrow aloud and ask these *either/or* questions:
- Is this a home or a classroom?
- Are there sixteen people or six people?
- Are there two women or three women?
- Are there three men or two men?
- Are there three children or two children?
- Are the people happy or sad?

Caption
- Read the photo caption aloud several times and have learners repeat it after you.
- Ask learners to tell you what they think the unit will be about.

Show photos of your family or pictures from magazines depicting family visits. Have learners tell you what they see.

Extension
Using the photo and the answers to the questions above, write a class story. Follow the suggestions on p. 8 for writing class stories.

32 **Unit 2**

Picture Dictionary

Follow the suggestions on p. 6 for introducing vocabulary.

Follow the suggestions on p. 6 for using vocabulary cards. Use the Vocabulary Card Masters for the words in the Picture Dictionary.

Activity A

Have learners copy the words and then copy them again into their notebooks.

- Circulate to check learners' work.
- Point to the words randomly and ask learners to say them.
- Point to the words randomly and ask learners to spell them.

One Step Up

Some learners may be ready to learn the plural forms of the words in the Picture Dictionary.

- Write the words that have regular plurals on the board. To practice singular forms, write a numeral 1 before each word. Say each word and have learners repeat it.
- Next, erase each number 1 and write 2, 3, 4, 5 before each word. Add an *s* to each word. Say each word and have learners repeat it.
- Have learners tape word cards under the correct column on the board—*singular* or *plural*.
- Point out to learners that the plural forms of *man* and *woman* are exceptions to the rule. Note also the spelling change in *wives*.
- Write these plural forms.
- Point out the difference in pronunciation between the singular and plural forms.

In the US

In the US, the words *restroom, bathroom,* and *men's* or *women's room* are often used interchangeably. However, not all restrooms use the universal icons for male and female. If possible, show learners pictures of restroom doors to ensure comprehension.

Activity B

Have learners write the words in alphabetical order.

Answers
1. daughter   3. son   5. woman
2. husband   4. wife

Extension

Make vocabulary cards using the words in the word box. Then do this activity:

- After learners have written the words in alphabetical order in their notebooks, give vocabulary cards to five of them and have them arrange themselves in alphabetical order according to their cards. Repeat this several times.
- Have learners tape the cards to the board in alphabetical order. Then practice spelling the words together aloud.

Use Customizable Master 1 (Bingo Chart). See p. 8 for how to play Bingo with vocabulary words.

Remember Box

Write the alphabet on the board as learners call out the letters in order.

Extension

Play Concentration with the vocabulary cards as a review. Use the Vocabulary Card Masters for the words in the Picture Dictionary. See game directions on p. 9.

Unit 2 33

Lesson 1: Family Photos

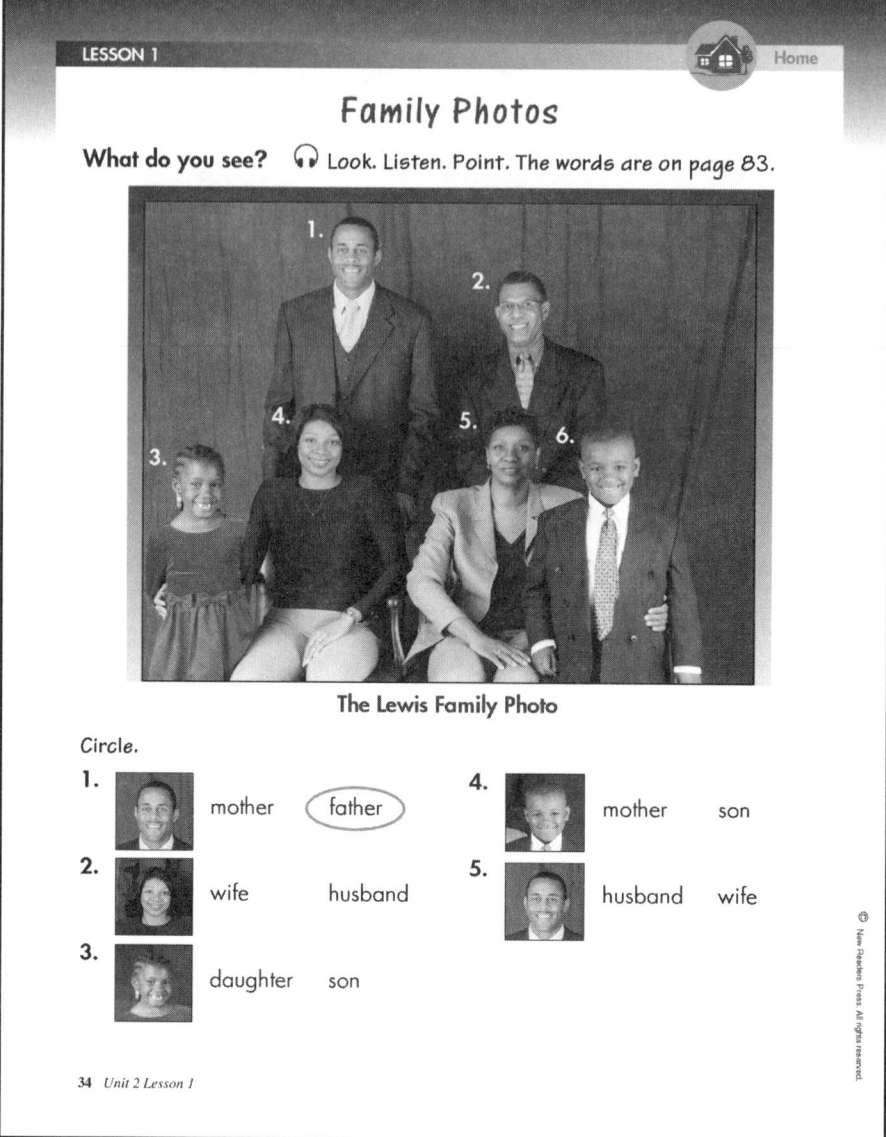

Photo
Follow the suggestions on p. 5 for talking about the photo. Ask these questions:
- Who are the people?
- Where are they?
- How do they feel?
- What are the men doing?
- What are the women doing?
- What are the children doing?

Caption
- Have learners repeat the caption several times.
- Ask questions about the people to review family vocabulary from p. 33. Point to each person and ask, "Who is this?"

Listening
The audio program uses the numbers on the Lewis Family photo to describe the family relationships. Play the audio or read the listening script below as learners point to each person in the photo. Repeat several times.

Listening Script
Look. Listen. Point.
One: I'm a husband. I'm a father.
Two: I'm a husband. I'm a grandfather.
Three: I'm a daughter. I'm a sister.
Four: I'm a wife. I'm a mother.
Five: I'm a wife. I'm a grandmother.
Six: I'm a son. I'm a brother.

Extensions
1. Bring a camera to class and do the following:
   - Say, "I'm a photographer."
   - Have learners pose for a group photo. Ask them to "Smile!" as you take a picture.
   - Make copies of the photo for each learner or for a classroom display.
   - Have learners count the number of people in the photo.
2. Have partners take turns dictating family words to each other.
3. Follow these steps to demonstrate family words:
   - Have learners ask you, "Who are you?"
   - Reply using as many appropriate family words as possible in your responses (e.g., "I'm Mike Garcia's son. I'm Linda Garcia's brother . . . ."
   - Have learners work in pairs to ask and answer the same question.

Comprehension
Follow the suggestions on p. 6 for listening/reading comprehension.

Answers
1. father
2. wife
3. daughter
4. son
5. husband

Picture Dictionary

Follow the suggestions on p. 6 for introducing vocabulary.

Follow the suggestions on p. 6 for using vocabulary cards. Use the Vocabulary Card Masters for the words in the Picture Dictionary.

To establish the meaning of *grand* and *child,* do the following:
- Write the word part *grand* on six vocabulary cards. Tape them to the board.
- Tape the cards for *mother, father, son,* and *daughter* next to the first four *grand* cards.
- Make two more cards, each with *child* on it.
- Point to the photo of the grandson and say *child*. Do the same with the photo of the granddaughter to show that *child* is used for both boys and girls.

Activity A

Before learners do this activity, have them read the pairs of words for each numbered item. Then play the audio or read the words while learners circle the words they hear.

Listening Script/Answers
Listen. Circle.
1. grandmother   3. grandchild
2. granddaughter   4. Mr. Lewis

Class Chat

Use Customizable Master 3 (3-Column Chart). Follow the suggestions on p. 7 (Preparing for a Class Chat) for customizing and duplicating the master and distributing the copies.

Follow the suggestions on p. 7 for facilitating Class Chats.

Extensions
1. Have learners write sentences using the information from the chat (e.g., *Mr. Radich is married.*). Then have them read their sentences to a partner.

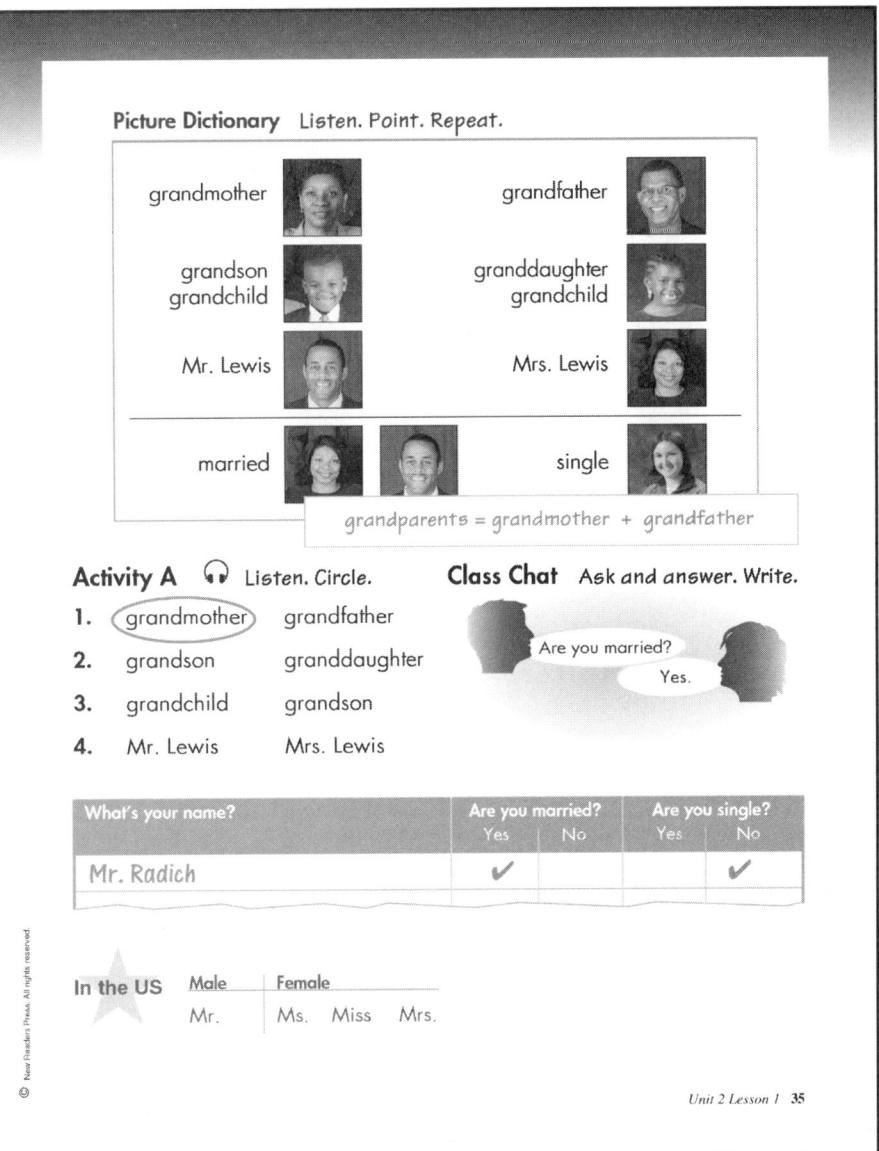

2. Bring photos of your family to class to share with learners:
   - Have them ask you questions about the photos.
   - Ask them to bring their own photos to class to share.

If some learners do not have family photos to share with the class, have them draw pictures of their family or give them "new families"—pictures you have cut from magazines.

In the US

Have learners identify themselves as Mr., Mrs., Miss, or Ms.

Use Unit Master 18 (Life Skills: Who Are You?) now or at any time during the rest of the unit.

Use Customizable Master 1 (Bingo Chart). Follow the suggestions on p. 8 for playing Vocabulary Bingo.

Unit 2 *Lesson 1* 35

Vocabulary

Follow the suggestions on p. 6 for introducing vocabulary.

Follow the suggestions on p. 6 for using vocabulary cards. Use the Vocabulary Card Masters for the words in the Vocabulary box.

Activity B

Play the audio or say the numbers while learners write the numerals for what they hear.

<u>Listening Script/Answers</u>
Listen. Write numbers.
a. 27   c. 21   e. 26   g. 30   i. 29
b. 23   d. 28   f. 24   h. 22   j. 25

<u>One Step Up</u>
Have learners write the words for each number in Activity B.

Activity C

Review the suggestions for Pair Dictations on p. 8. Circulate to monitor learners while they dictate and write the numbers. Make sure they do not look at the answers.

Task 1

Use Customizable Master 5 (Idea Map). Write the words *My Family* in the circle. Make a copy for each learner. If learners come from large families, tell them to draw additional circles on their idea maps.

One Step Up

Have more advanced learners count the number of people in their families. This is a good way to review numbers, especially if learners come from large families.

<u>Extension</u>
Play Concentration with vocabulary cards, matching numbers with the words for numbers to make a set (e.g., *23* with *twenty-three*). Use the Vocabulary Card Masters for numbers 21–30. See directions for Concentration on p. 9.

 Assign Workbook pp. 22–24.

36   Unit 2 *Lesson 1*

Vocabulary   Listen. Point. Repeat.

21	22	23	24	25
twenty-one	twenty-two	twenty-three	twenty-four	twenty-five
26	27	28	29	30
twenty-six	twenty-seven	twenty-eight	twenty-nine	thirty

Activity B   Listen. Write numbers.

a. <u>27</u>   c. ____   e. ____   g. ____   i. ____
b. ____   d. ____   f. ____   h. ____   j. ____

Activity C   Listen to a partner. Don't look. Write.

Partner A Speaks	Partner B Writes	Partner B Speaks	Partner A Writes
1. 22	twenty-two	1. 23	_____
2. 27	_____	2. 29	_____
3. 21	_____	3. 26	_____
4. 30	_____	4. 28	_____
5. 24	_____	5. 25	_____

 TASK 1   Your Family

Write about your family in your notebook.

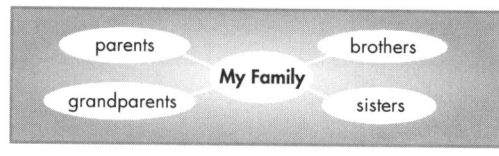

One Step Up
How many people are in your family? Count. Circle *a, b, c,* or *d.*

a) 1–10
b) 11–20
c) 21–30
d) 30+

Lesson 2: Your ID, Please

Photos

Follow the suggestions on p. 5 for talking about the photos and photo caption.

Then ask these questions:

Photo 1
- Where is Mr. Lewis?
- Is he at work or at home?
- What is he holding?
- Is it a camera or a photo?

Photo 2
- What is Mr. Lewis doing?
- Is he sitting or standing?
- Is he looking at a photo or a computer?

Photo 3
- What is Mr. Lewis doing?
- Is he sitting or standing?
- Is he smiling?

Photo 4
- What is Mr. Lewis doing?
- Is he happy or sad?
- What is he holding? (*an ID*)

Read the speech and thought bubbles several times while learners point to the pictures.

Attention Box

This vocabulary should be understood, but learners should not be expected to produce the words at this point.
- Establish the meaning of *love* by drawing a large heart on the board.
- Hold up a blank piece of paper. Pick up another one, and another, and another—each time saying the word *more*.
- Draw two smiling faces on the board. Under one, write *like*. Draw an *x* through the second face to show *don't like*. Then show learners pictures of things you like and don't like.
- Show the same pictures again and ask learners to respond by saying *like* or *don't like*.

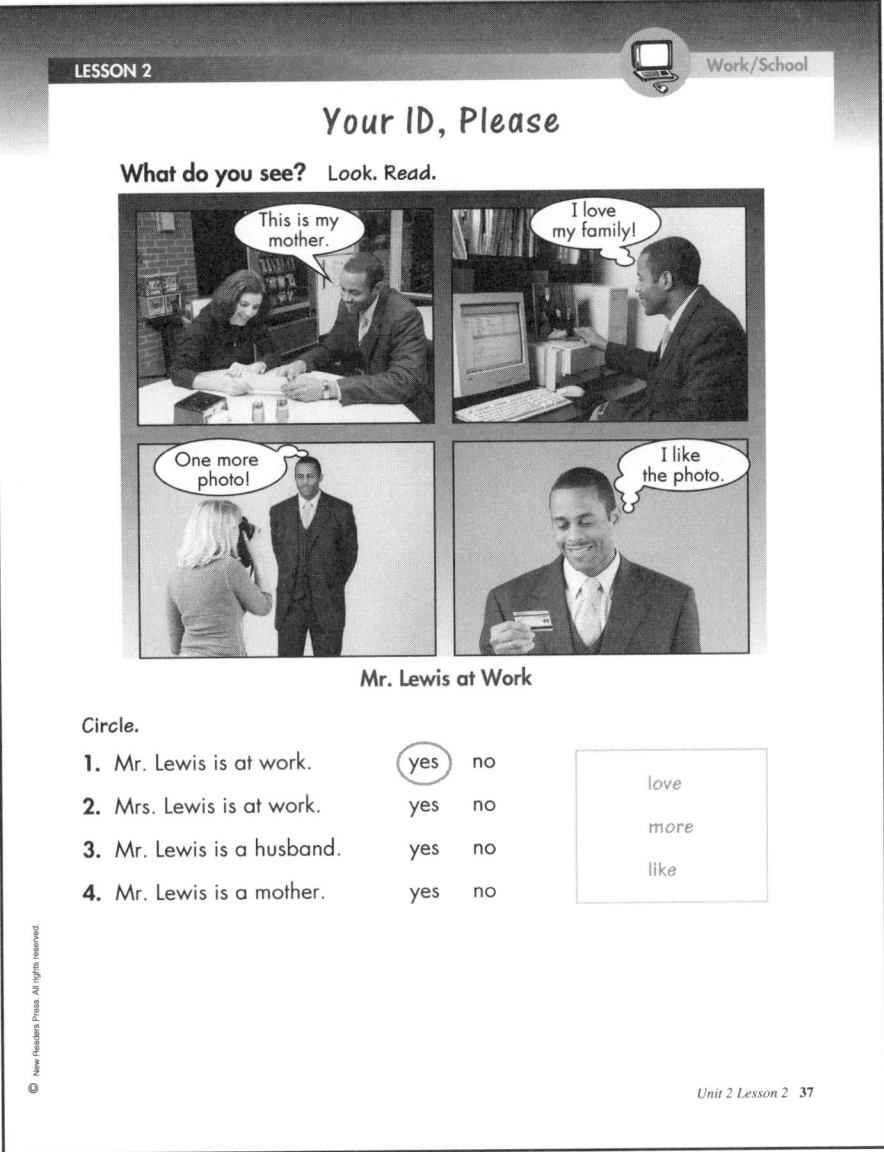

Comprehension

Follow the suggestions on p. 6 for listening/reading comprehension.

Answers
1. yes   2. no   3. yes   4. no

Unit 2 *Lesson 2* 37

Vocabulary

Follow the suggestions on p. 6 for introducing vocabulary.

Follow the suggestions on p. 6 for using vocabulary cards. Use the Vocabulary Card Masters for the words in the Vocabulary box.

Extension
To provide additional practice with the vocabulary words, follow these steps:
- Draw a large facsimile of the photo ID on the board, poster board, or easel paper.
- Give the vocabulary cards to learners.
- Have learners tape the cards on the correct places on the ID (e.g., put a vocabulary card with *ID number* on the place that reads 27-15-4-30).

In the US

Area codes are often written in two different ways—with parentheses and without. Point out to learners that both ways are correct.

Have learners clap out the rhythm of phone numbers with area codes.

Activity A

Have learners complete the matching activity. Next, call out each number and ask a learner to say the letter of his or her answer. If an incorrect answer is given, continue to ask until the correct one is provided. Explain or demonstrate why that answer is correct.

Answers
1. d   3. c   5. h   7. f
2. b   4. a   6. g   8. e

Activity B

Before learners ask and answer questions about the ID, model what you want them to do. Circulate while learners practice, and monitor their work.

Vocabulary Listen. Point. Repeat.

ID number	27-15-4-30	street address	1621 Green Street
area code	(630)	city	Blue Lake
phone number	555-8518	state	IL
e-mail address	blewis@brown.com	zip code	60135

Brown Brothers Company
1621 Green Street
Blue Lake, IL 60135
(630) 555-8518

Benjamin Lewis
Computer Programmer
ID: 27-15-4-30
blewis@brown.com

St. = Street
Dr. = Drive
Ave. = Avenue

In the US (630) 555-8518 = 630-555-8518

Activity A Match.
1. ID number
2. area code
3. address
4. zip code
5. state
6. phone number
7. city
8. e-mail address

a. 60135
b. (630)
c. 1621 Green Street
d. 27-15-4-30
e. blewis@brown.com
f. Blue Lake
g. 555-8518
h. IL

Activity B Look at Ben's ID card. Talk to a partner. Ask questions with words in Activity A.

One Step Up
Talk about you.
Student A: Zip code?
Student B: 60139

One Step Up

Since it is likely that several learners in a group will have the same zip code, make cards with additional zip codes for learners to practice numbers. Use real zip codes for your area.

Attention Box

The focus here is on using polite language—*excuse me, please, thank you/thanks,* and *you're welcome.* Ask individual learners to hand you various objects in the classroom. Use the polite words from the box as you ask for and receive them.

In the US

Encourage learners to use clarification language *(Excuse me?)* when they do not understand or want something repeated.

Follow the suggestions on p. 5 for talking about the photo.
Ask these questions:
• Who do you see?
• Where are they?
• What is Ben doing?

Play the audio or read the dialogue printed on the page. Have learners repeat after you before they practice with a partner.

Class Chat

Use Customizable Master 3 (3-Column Chart). Follow the suggestions on p. 7 (Preparing for a Class Chat) for customizing and duplicating the master and distributing the copies.

Follow the suggestions on p. 7 for facilitating Class Chats.

Class Chat Follow-Up

Have learners read their sentences to you, a partner, a small group, or the class.

If there is concern about security or privacy, give learners index cards with the names of streets in the community to use instead of their own addresses.

Point out that for street addresses without house numbers, *on* is used (e.g., *Julio lives on Maple Street*). *At* is used for addresses that

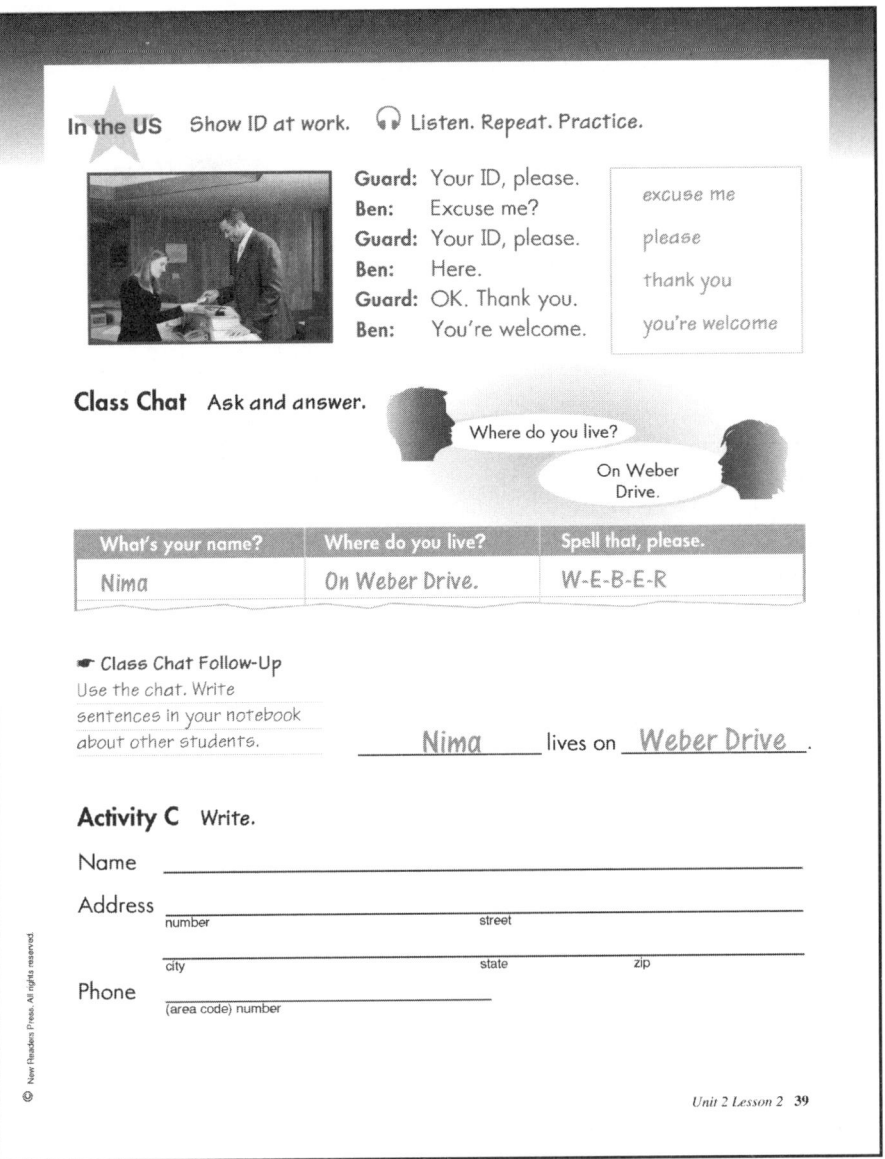

include both a house number and a street name (e.g., *Maya lives at 276 Elm Street*).

Activity C

While learners are writing, circulate to monitor their work. Point at random to words an individual learner is writing on the form and have the learner say them. Then ask questions such as, "What's your phone number?"

Tell learners that if they have an apartment number, they need to include it after the street address.

Extensions
1. Since it is vital for learners to know their personal information, give them small index cards and have them copy the information from this activity onto the cards. If possible, laminate the cards and encourage learners to put them in their wallets.
2. Have learners work in pairs to ask and answer questions about the forms. If learners seem reluctant to share this information, prepare cards for them to use.

Unit 2 Lesson 2 39

Language

Follow the suggestions on p. 6 for introducing vocabulary. Notice that the personal pronouns are used here only as words to be read, not as grammatical items.

Extension

Show learners pictures of people and ask them to say the correct pronoun.

Activity D

Follow the suggestions for reading activities on p. 6. Read the stories aloud several times.

Answers

Mr. Lewis's Story:
1. married   2. husband

Mrs. Lewis's Story:
1. mother   2. yes   3. yes

Task 2

Before learners begin Task 2, model the task:
- Draw a large square on the board.
- Draw a picture of yourself in the square.
- Write sentences about yourself on the board or on an overhead transparency. Follow the patterns in the stories in Activity D above.
- Read your sentences to learners.
- Have learners read the sentences to you.

Use Unit Masters 19 (Reading: The Letter *M*), 20 (Reading: The Letter *N*), and 21 (Game: Tell Me the Answer) now or at any time during the rest of the unit.

Unit Master 21

To play this game, put learners in groups of no more than four.
- Give each learner a game piece and a coin to flip. The object of the game is to flip a coin and move one space for heads or two for tails. Learners must read the box and give the correct information. The first person to make it around the board is the winner.
- Model how to play so learners understand what to do.

Assign Workbook pages 25–27.

Activity D Read. Write.

Mr. Lewis's Story
He is Ben Lewis.
He is married.
He is a husband.
He is a father.

1. Is he married or single? _____married_____
2. Is he a husband or a wife? _____

Mrs. Lewis's Story
She is Michelle Lewis.
She is married.
She is a wife.
She is a mother.

1. Is she a father or a mother? _____
2. Is she Mr. Lewis's wife? _____
3. Are they married? _____

Language

I
you
he
she
they

TASK 2   Your Story
Draw. Write.

I am _____.
I am _____.
I am a _____.
I am a _____.
My address is _____.
My phone number is _____.

Unit 2 Project

Learners apply the vocabulary and concepts from the unit to create a family address book. Since it is unlikely that learners will have this information with them, the second step (Do the Work) will have to be done as homework.

Get Ready

Duplicate and distribute Customizable Master 3 (3-Column Chart). Have two copies available for each learner.

Do the Work

Have learners make a family address book at home and bring it to the next class.

Present Your Project

- Have learners take turns writing names from their address books.
- Have learners ask questions about the names in each other's address books. This can be an informal review of family words.

<u>One Step Up</u>

Learners who have e-mail accounts can add their e-mail addresses to their address books. Give learners your e-mail address and encourage them to write to you. The messages can be as simple as, "Hi. I am Jose. How are you today?"

Technology Extra

You may want to set up a chart template into which learners can type their family address book information.

Assign Workbook p. 28: Check Your Progress.

Use Unit Master 22 (Unit 2 Checkup/Review) whenever you complete this unit.

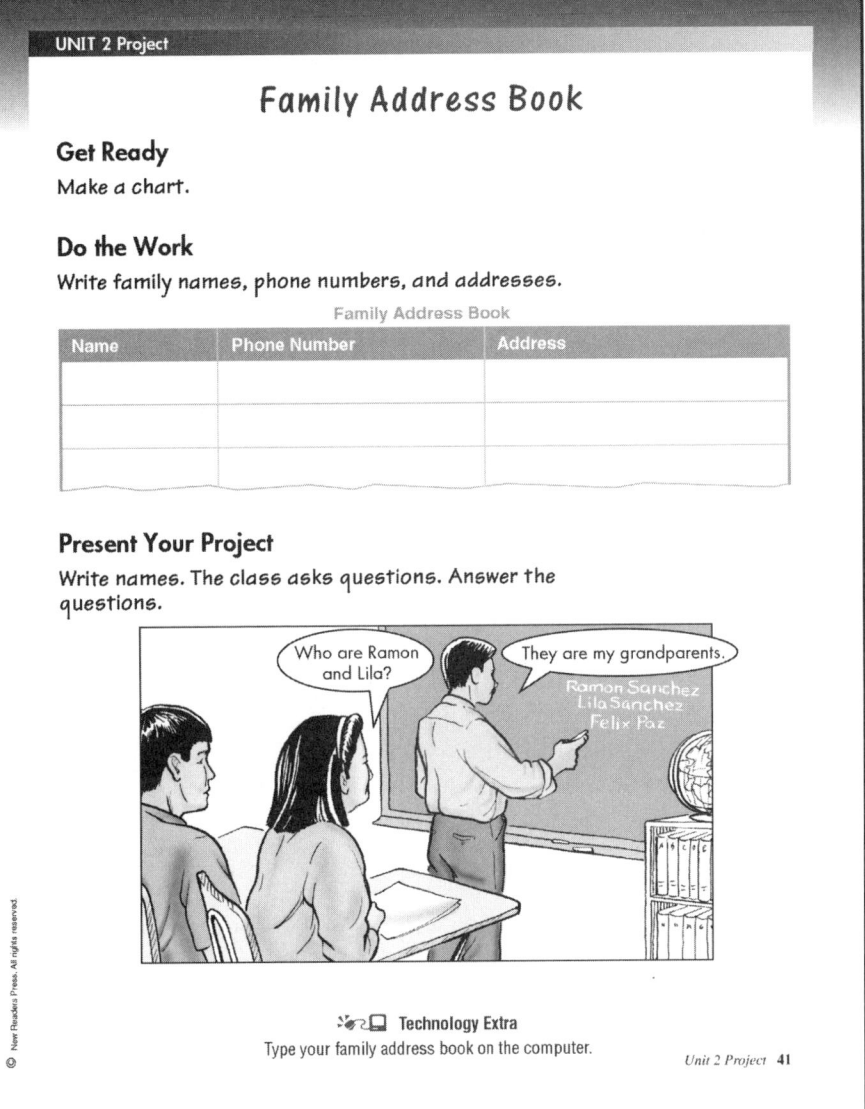

Unit 3: You're Sick

Materials for the Unit
- Vocabulary Card Masters for Unit 3
- Various calendars
- Clocks, clock cards, or a clock facsimile
- Thermometer for checking a person's temperature (or an illustration of a thermometer)
- Unit Masters 23–28
- Customizable Masters 1, 2, 4, 6
- Generic Assessment Masters 7, 8

You're Sick
Follow these steps to discuss the unit title:
- Pantomime being sick by doubling over, grimacing, or doing whatever else will demonstrate the concept.
- With a frown, say, "I'm sick."
- On the board, write *fine* with a smiling face by it and *sick* with a frowning face by it.
- Ask learners, "Are you fine or are you sick?"
- When someone says "Sick," respond sympathetically with "You're sick."
- Point out the phrase *you're sick* in the book.
- Use a medical thermometer as a prop to demonstrate the concept *sick*.
- Have learners repeat the phrase "You're sick."

Photo
Follow the suggestions on p. 5 for talking about the photo.

Read the question below the arrow aloud and ask these *either/or* questions:
- Is this a house or an office?
- Is she a girl or a boy?
- Is the girl fine or sick?
- Point to the woman entering the room and ask, "Is she a mother or a father?"
- Point to the woman in the smock and ask, "Is she a teacher or a nurse?"

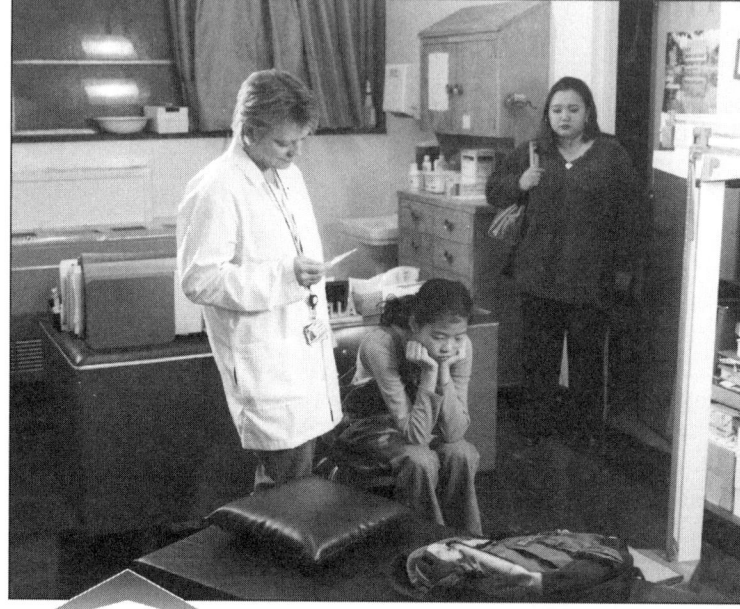

My daughter is sick.

What do you see?

Caption
- Read the photo caption several times and have learners repeat it after you.
- Have them tell you what they think the unit will be about. This fosters learner comprehension as well as predicting skills. It also helps learners build a reference for the unit.

Picture Dictionary

Follow the suggestions on p. 6 for introducing vocabulary.

Follow the suggestions on p. 6 for using vocabulary cards. Use the Vocabulary Card Masters for the words in the Picture Dictionary.

If possible, bring in and point to real objects to demonstrate the words *calendar, chair, clock,* and *thermometer.*

Activity A

Have learners write the words pictured and then copy the words into their notebooks.
- Circulate to check learners' work.
- Point to the words randomly and ask learners to say them.
- Point to the words randomly and ask learners to spell them.

Answers
1. girl   3. chair
2. nurse   4. thermometer

Extensions
1. Point to a variety of objects. Try to elicit roughly the same number of *yes* and *no* answers as you ask questions like these:
   - Is this a clock? (point to a chair)
     Learners: No!
   - Is this a chair? (point to a chair)
     Learners: Yes!
2. After some practice with direct questions, ask *either/or* questions.
   - Is this a calendar or a clock?
     Learners: A calendar.
   - Is this a nurse or a student?
     Learners: A nurse.
3. Have learners work in pairs, using their vocabulary cards in these ways:
   - One partner shows a card. The other says the word.
   - To practice spelling, one partner asks, "How do you spell _____?" The other spells the word.

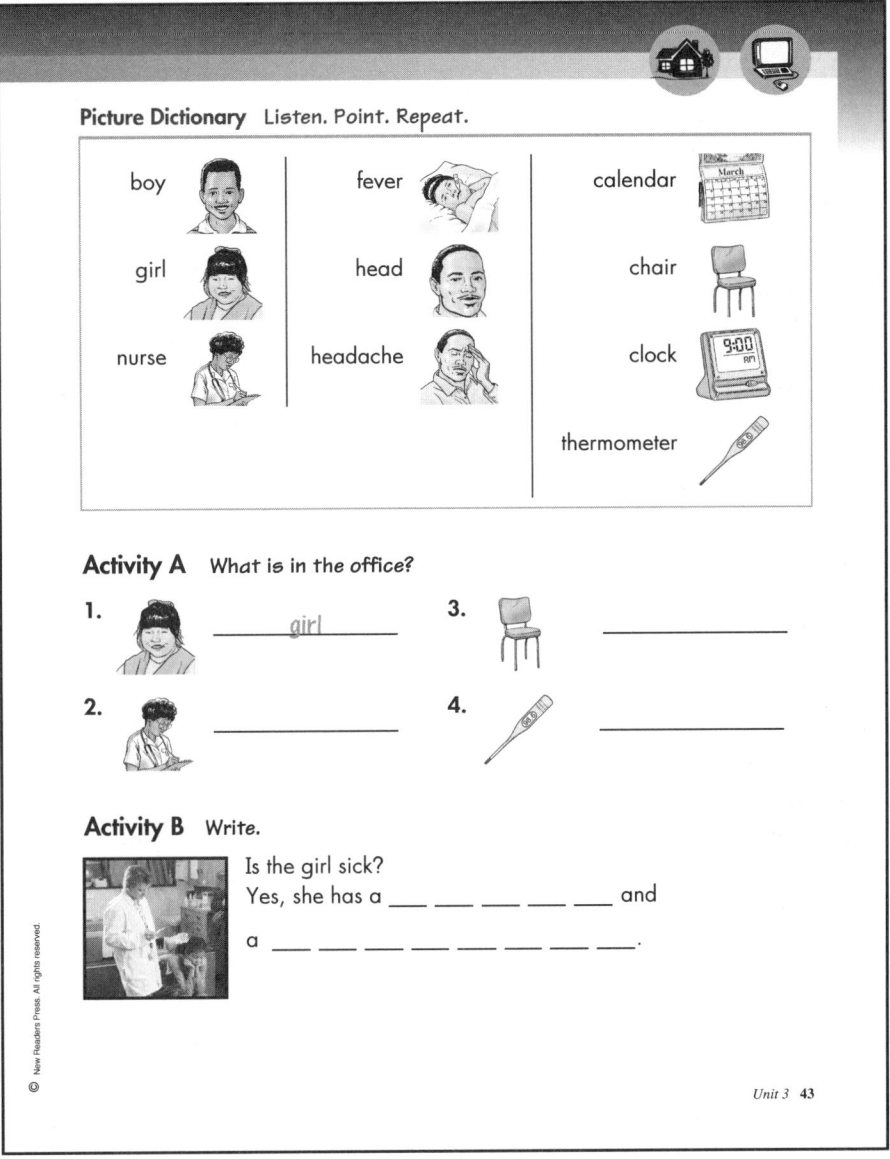

Circulate to monitor the pair practice.

Activity B

First do the activity orally.
- Ask learners, "Is the girl's head hot?" Pantomime the sensation of heat as you touch your own forehead.
- Ask, "Does she have a fever?" Lead the learners in answering *yes* and stating, "She has a fever."
- Using the same pantomime, ask, "Does she have a headache?"

Next, have learners write the missing words and then copy them into their notebooks:
- Circulate while learners are writing, and monitor their work.
- Point to the words randomly and ask learners to say them.

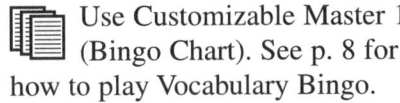 Use Customizable Master 1 (Bingo Chart). See p. 8 for how to play Vocabulary Bingo.

Unit 3 43

Lesson 1: Your Daughter Is Sick

Remember Box

Ask if someone can read the words *daughter* and *mother*. If many have forgotten the words, write *father* and *son* on the board. Point to learners who have children to show examples of *mother* and *father*.

Photos

Follow the suggestions on p. 5 for talking about photos. Ask these questions to help establish meaning:
- Are the people on the telephone?
- Who is this? (pointing to the nurse) Is the nurse at school?
- Who is this? (pointing to Dyna) Is Dyna at school? Is she at home?
- Is Dyna happy?

Listening

Play the audio or read the listening script below several times. Have learners point to the person who is speaking. After they have listened, point to the nurse and ask, "Who is this?" Do the same for Dyna.

Next ask, "Who is sick?" and "What's wrong?" You should expect only one-word answers. Because the lesson focuses on vocabulary acquisition and not grammar, it is not necessary for learners to produce complete sentences at this point.

Play the audio or read the listening script again and ask learners to repeat what they hear. Circulate to monitor their work while they listen and repeat.

Listening Script
What do you see? Look. Listen. Point.
Nurse: Your daughter is sick.
Dyna: What's wrong?
Nurse: She has a fever.
Dyna: Excuse me? Please repeat.
Nurse: A fever.
Dyna: Oh. I see.

Attention Box

Mime *fine* vs. *sick*. Ask if a learner is fine or sick. Go around the room asking a number of learners the same question.

Next ask, "Who is sick today?" and "Who is fine today?"

Comprehension

Have learners answer the questions at the bottom of the page. Allow them to do so without prompting if they can. Otherwise, play the audio or read the listening script with them.

Answers
1. no   3. no   5. no
2. yes   4. yes   6. yes

Picture Dictionary

Follow the suggestions on p. 6 for introducing vocabulary.

Follow the suggestions on p. 6 for using vocabulary cards. Use the Vocabulary Card Masters for the words in the Picture Dictionary.

- Draw a large frontal outline of a person.
- Pass out the vocabulary cards, one per person.
- Ask individual learners to tape their cards to the corresponding body parts on the drawing.
- Pass out vocabulary cards and have learners tape their cards to the board in alphabetical (ABC) order.
- Have learners copy the words in ABC order into their notebooks.

Activity A

Before learners begin this activity, do the following:
- Read the listening script below or have learners listen to the audio at least twice. Ask them to write the words on the lines as they hear them.
- Play the audio or read the script again and have learners check their own work or a partner's.

Listening Script/Answers
Listen. Write.
1. head   6. eye
2. nose   7. ear
3. mouth   8. stomach
4. arm   9. hand
5. foot   10. leg

Use Customizable Master 1 (Bingo Chart). See p. 8 for how to play Vocabulary Bingo.

Use Unit Master 23 (Game: Make a Face) now or at any time during the rest of the unit.

Have learners work in pairs. Duplicate one master per pair—or one per person if you do the activity twice. Follow these steps:

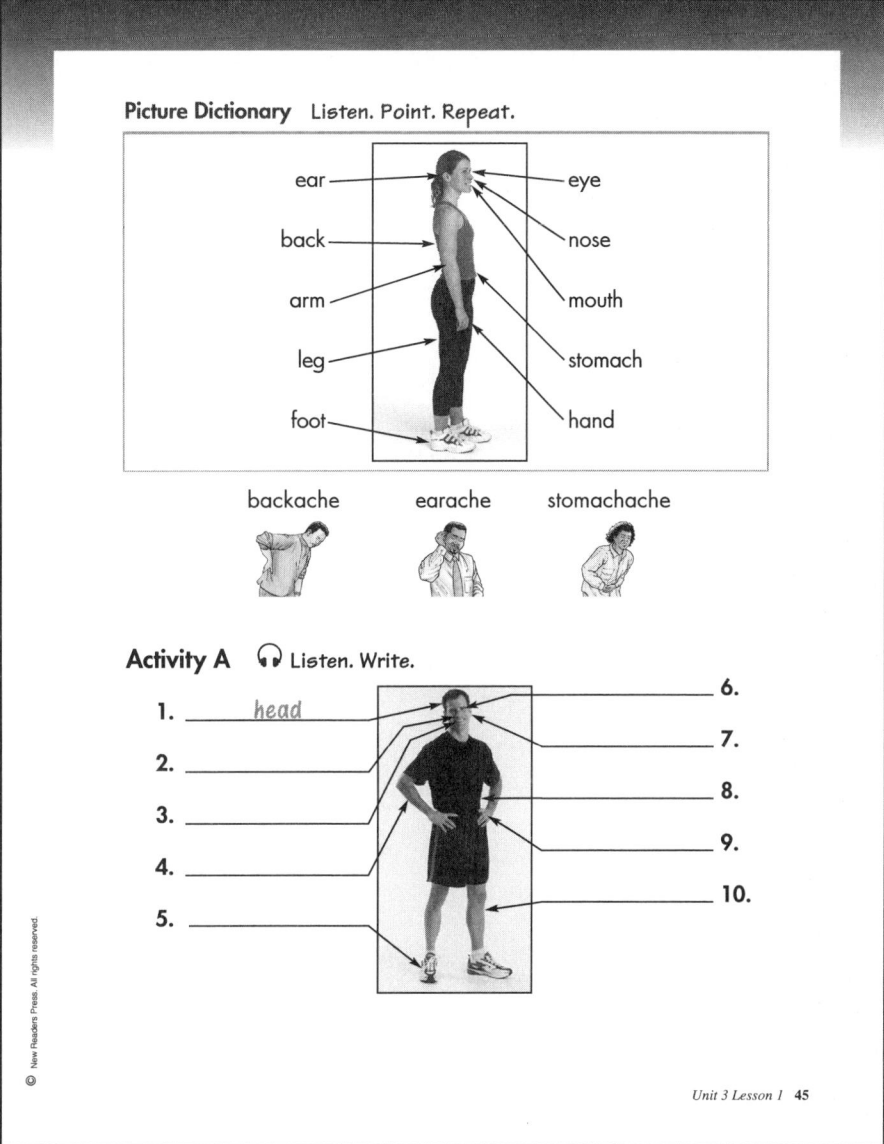

1. Cut out the outlined face and give it to one of the partners. Then cut out the eyes, ears, nose, and mouth and give them to the other partner. (If you have enough scissors, make the cutting a class activity.)
2. Have learners ask for a number and position the corresponding body part in its proper place on the face. Follow these examples:
   - What's number one?
   - It's an eye. Here's the eye.
   - What's number five?
   - It's the nose. Here's the nose.

Extension
Have learners color parts of the face following instructions given by you or their partners. Or, have learners draw silly facial features to create cartoon-like faces.

Unit 3 *Lesson 1* 45

Partner Chat

Have learners work in pairs. One learner asks, "What is this?" while pointing to a body part. The other names the body part.
- Model the activity by asking one learner, who gives the answer.
- Have two learners model the activity.
- Ask partners to take turns asking and answering at least four times.

Extension

Lead learners in a game of Simon Says.
- Begin by asking learners to touch a part of their body: "Put your hand on your head."
- Once learners are able to follow the instructions correctly, play Simon Says. Tell learners to respond only when Simon asks them to do something.
- Say, "Put your hand on your arm." (No response.)
- Say, "Simon says put your hand on your arm." (Learners put their hands on their arms.)

Activity B

Play the audio or read the listening script below several times. Have learners do the following:
- Point to the various body parts as they listen.
- Circle the words they hear.
- Call out the answers to each item when they finish the activity.
- Play the audio or read the listening script again and ask learners to check their answers.

Listening Script/Answers

Listen. Circle. What's wrong?
1. My head hurts.
   What hurts?
   My head.
2. O-oh [moan], my leg.
   What's wrong?
   My leg hurts.
3. I have a stomachache.
   Where does it hurt?
   Here in my stomach.
4. Ouch! My hand.
   What hurts?
   My hand!
5. Mommy . . . my eye hurts.
   What's wrong, honey?
   My eye hurts.

One Step Up

Have learners fill in the missing letters.

Answers
head   mouth
foot   leg
arm   hand
back   ear

Task 1

Learners who have children should use the personal information for one child to fill in the form. Assign them the task of finding and spelling their doctor's name, address, and telephone number.

Those who do not have children can use a relative's information or make up information to complete the form.

Extension

Play Concentration with vocabulary cards to review vocabulary. Use Vocabulary Card Masters for words introduced on pages 43 and 45. See directions for the game on p. 9.

 Assign Workbook pp. 29–31.

Lesson 2: Stay Home Today!

Follow the suggestions on p. 5 for talking about the photos and p. 6 for talking about the title.

Photos

Read the photo caption, "Dyna calls work," several times and have learners repeat it after you. Then ask these questions about the photos:

Photo 1
- Is Dyna at work or at home?
- What is she holding?
- What is she doing?
- Who is in the room with Dyna?
- Is her daughter fine or sick?
- What's wrong with her?

Photo 2
- Where is the woman? At home or in an office?
- Is she sitting or standing?
- What is she pointing to?
- Who is she?

Photo 3
- Is Dyna on the phone or on the computer?
- Is she happy or sad?

Photo 4
- What is the woman doing?
- What day is it?

Have learners read the sentences in the speech bubbles several times.

Attention Box

This vocabulary should be understood but learners should not be expected to write and memorize these words.

Follow these steps to aid comprehension:
- Establish the meaning of the word *today* by posting a large calendar in front of the learners.
- Point to the current day and repeat the word *today* several times.
- Point to the previous day and repeat the word *yesterday* several times.
- Do the same for *tomorrow*.

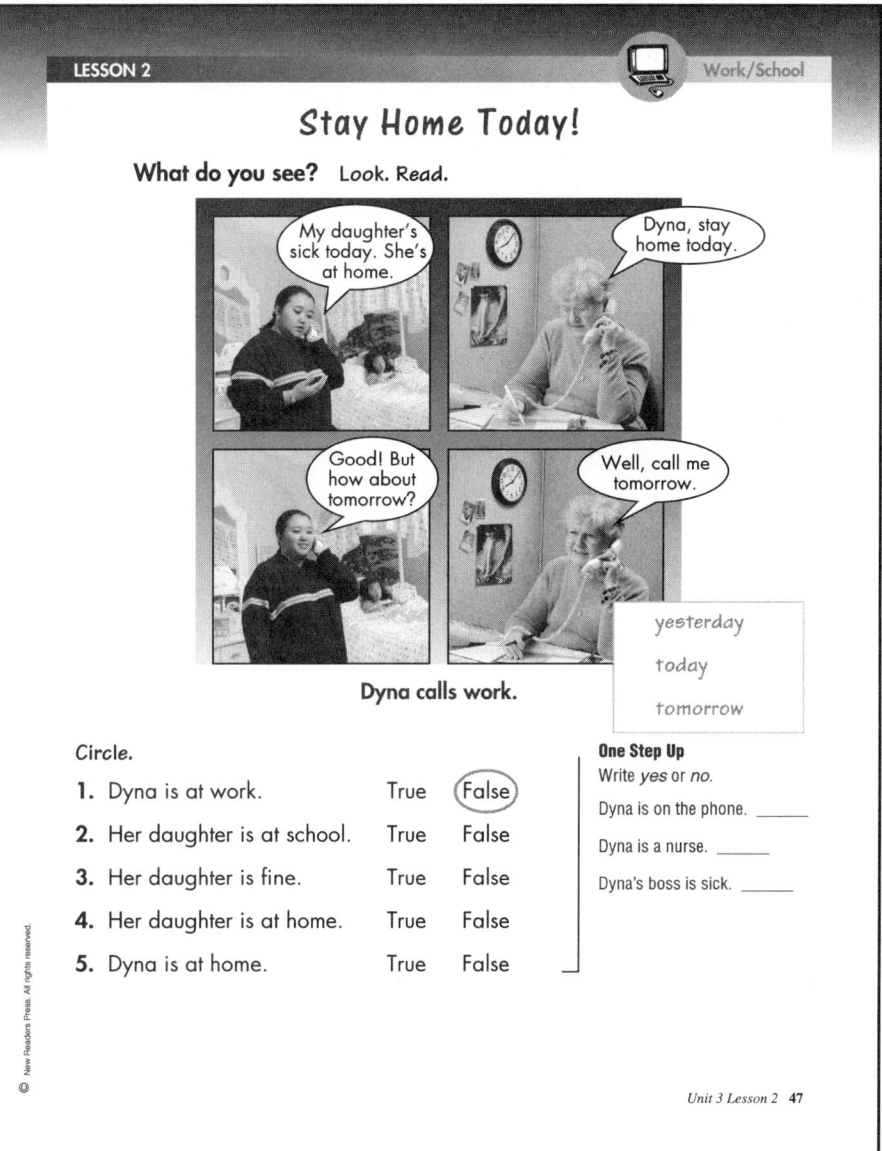

Comprehension

First explain that *true* means *yes* and *false* means *no*. If learners are able to work independently, have them complete the exercise. If not, make this a large-group activity by reading the sentences together.

Answers
1. False   3. False   5. True
2. False   4. True

Use Unit Master 24 (Reading: The Letter *B*) now or at any time during the rest of this unit.

Unit 3 *Lesson 2* 47

Vocabulary

Follow the suggestions on p. 6 for introducing vocabulary.

Follow the suggestions on p. 6 for using vocabulary cards. Use the Vocabulary Card Masters for the words in the Vocabulary box.

To provide additional practice with the words, follow these steps:
- Draw a large facsimile of a calendar on the board or on an overhead transparency.
- Label the calendar with the name of the current month.
- Ask learners to dictate the days of the week to you.
- Give vocabulary cards to learners.
- Have them tape the appropriate day in the corresponding space on the calendar.

Point out the pattern in the words (all end with the word *day*).

Tell learners that *Wednesday* is a long word, but it has only two syllables. Demonstrate this by clapping out the syllables. Practice the distinction between *Tuesday* (sounds like *two*) and *Thursday* (sounds like *thirty*).

Activity A

Designate learners as Partner A or Partner B. Ask the As to read the words while the Bs listen and circle the words they hear. Then have learners switch roles.

Activity B

Demonstrate the abbreviations for days of the week by showing learners a calendar that has the days in abbreviated form.
- Lead learners in this activity, matching days of the week with their abbreviations.
- After you do a few together as a group, they should be able to complete the rest on their own.

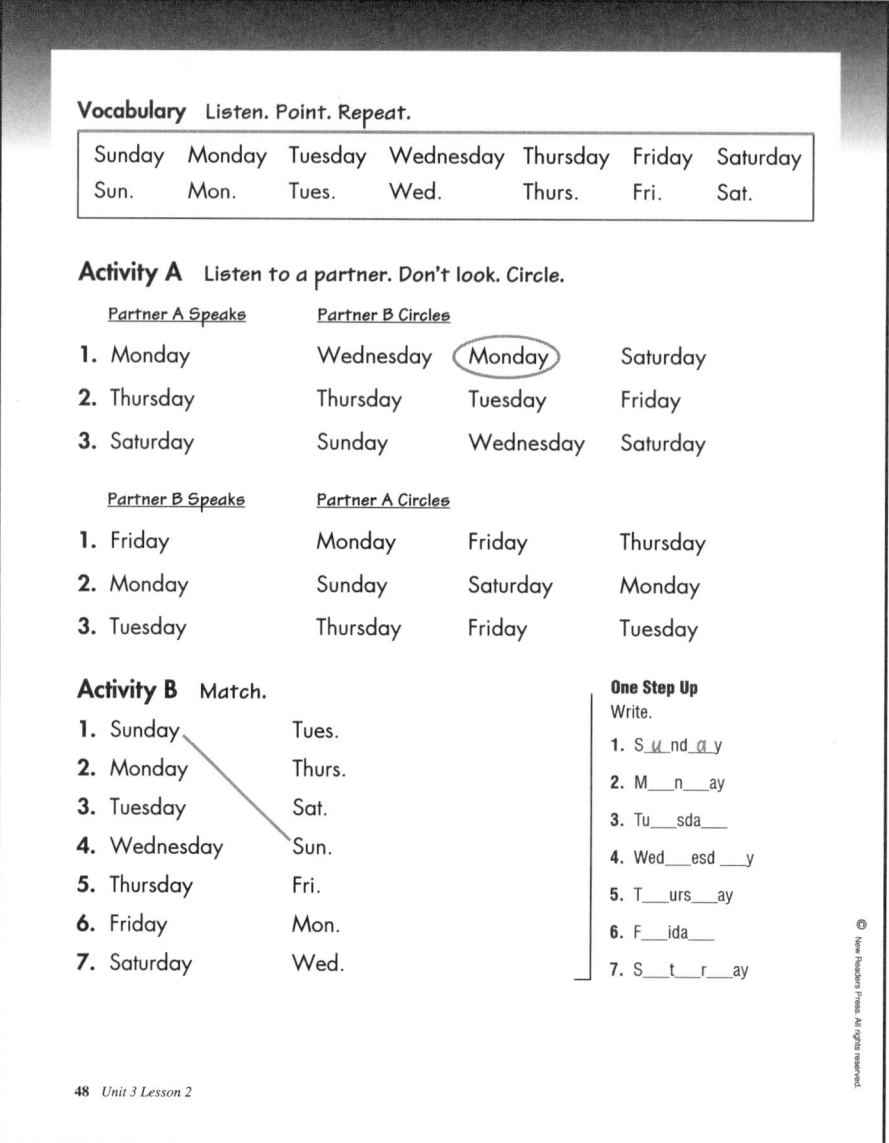

One Step Up

After learners have filled in the missing letters, ask those who have successfully completed the words to read them aloud.

Extension

More advanced learners can write the abbreviations for the days on their vocabulary cards next to or under the corresponding days of the week.

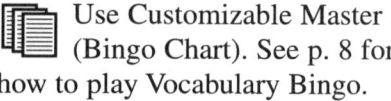 Use Unit Master 25 (Reading: The Letter *D*) now or at any time during the rest of this unit.

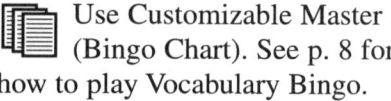 Use Customizable Master 1 (Bingo Chart). See p. 8 for how to play Vocabulary Bingo.

Extension

Play Concentration with vocabulary cards to review vocabulary. Use Vocabulary Card Masters for words introduced on pp. 43, 45, and 48. See directions for the game on p. 9.

48 Unit 3 *Lesson 2*

Picture Dictionary

Follow the suggestions on p. 6 for introducing vocabulary.

Follow the suggestions on p. 6 for using vocabulary cards. Use the Vocabulary Card Masters for the words in the Picture Dictionary.
- For the word *o'clock*, point out the apostrophe and demonstrate how to write it.
- Review the numbers through 30.
- As you teach the two new numbers *forty* and *fifty*, point out the difference in sound between *fourteen* and *forty*, and *fifteen* and *fifty*. Clap out the words, pointing out stressed syllables and how the stress differs in these pairs of words.
- Give learners a short dictation contrasting these pairs of numbers.
- Ask them to recite the numbers 1 through 50.
- Ask them to count to 50 by twos, by fives, and by tens.

Teach learners to tell time on a digital clock. (More complicated time-telling forms will be taught at the next level of *English—No Problem!*)

Use the vocabulary cards and a small clock on which you can easily change the time. Show how the first number represents the hour and the second number represents the minutes.

Class Chat

Create a page of digital clock faces showing a variety of times. Duplicate it and distribute one copy to each learner.
- Have learners listen and repeat the question, "What time is it?" several times.
- Have them circulate and ask each other the same question for each clock on their sheet.

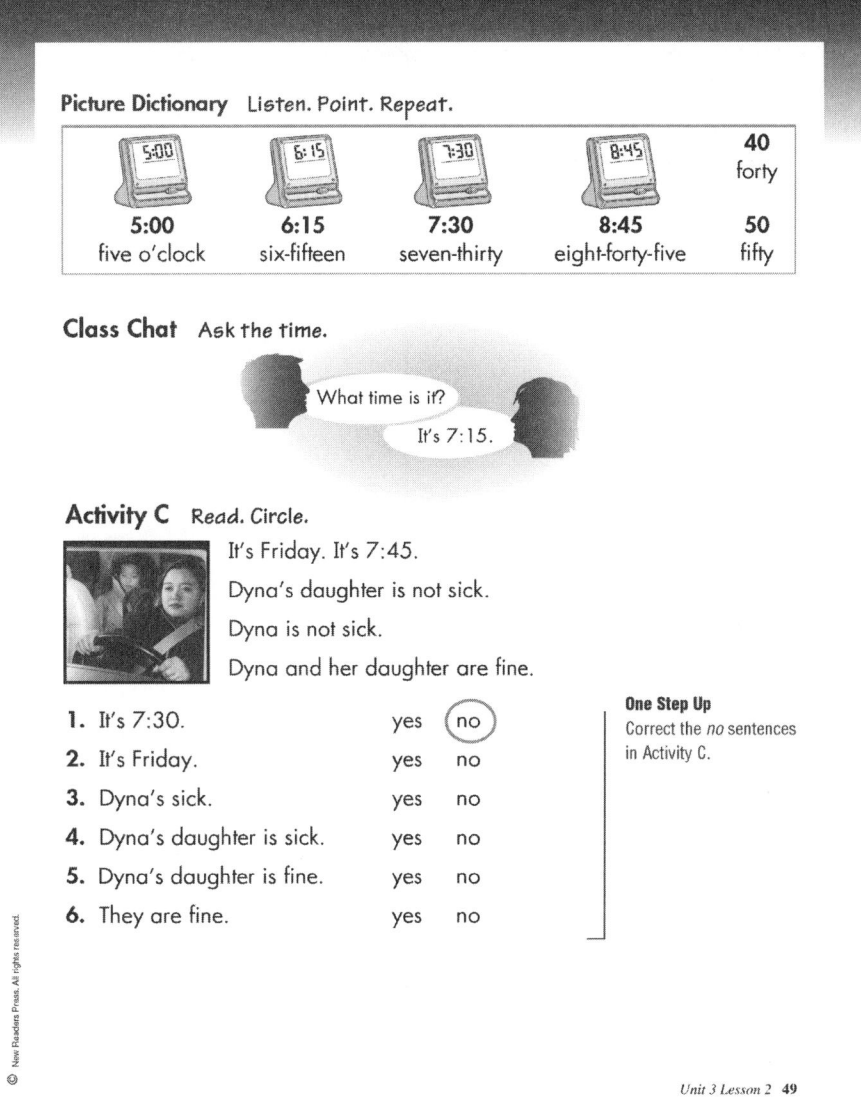

Activity C

Follow the suggestions on p. 5 for talking about the photo.
- Have learners read the four-line story silently. Allow independent readers to read the story and then do the comprehension activity.
- As an alternative, you or the learners can read the story and the sentences in the activity aloud.
- Then have learners circle *yes* or *no* working alone, in pairs, or as a whole group.

Answers
1. no   3. no   5. yes
2. yes   4. no   6. yes

One Step Up

Ask more advanced learners to correct the *no* sentences.

Answers
1. It's 7:45.
3. Dyna's fine.
4. Dyna's daughter is fine.

Unit 3 **Lesson 2** 49

In the US

Discuss these two scenarios:
1. It's Wednesday. You wake up. You are sick.
   <u>Question:</u> Can you go to work?
   <u>Answer:</u>   No! You have to call.
2. It's Wednesday. Your child wakes up. Your child is sick.
   <u>Question:</u> Can your child go to school?
   <u>Answer:</u>   No! Not with a fever. Call the school.

Activity D

Follow these steps:
- Model the conversation.
- Have learners repeat each line after you.
- Have two learners demonstrate the conversation.
- Have other learners practice the conversation in pairs.

Language

The focus should be on reading the words, not on mastering the grammatical forms.

This is learners' first exposure to forms of the verb *be*. Show them how some pronouns can be grouped—*he, she,* and *it* use *is*; *I* uses *am*.

Class Chat

 Use Customizable Master 4 (4-Column Chart).
- Make a copy of the master.
- Divide the columns in half, creating an eight-column chart.
- Follow the model in the student book for writing the column heads.
- Make copies and distribute them to learners.

Follow the suggestions on p. 7 for facilitating Class Chats.

<u>Extension</u>

Help learners write sentences based on the information in their Class Chat charts (e.g., *Po works on Monday and Friday*).

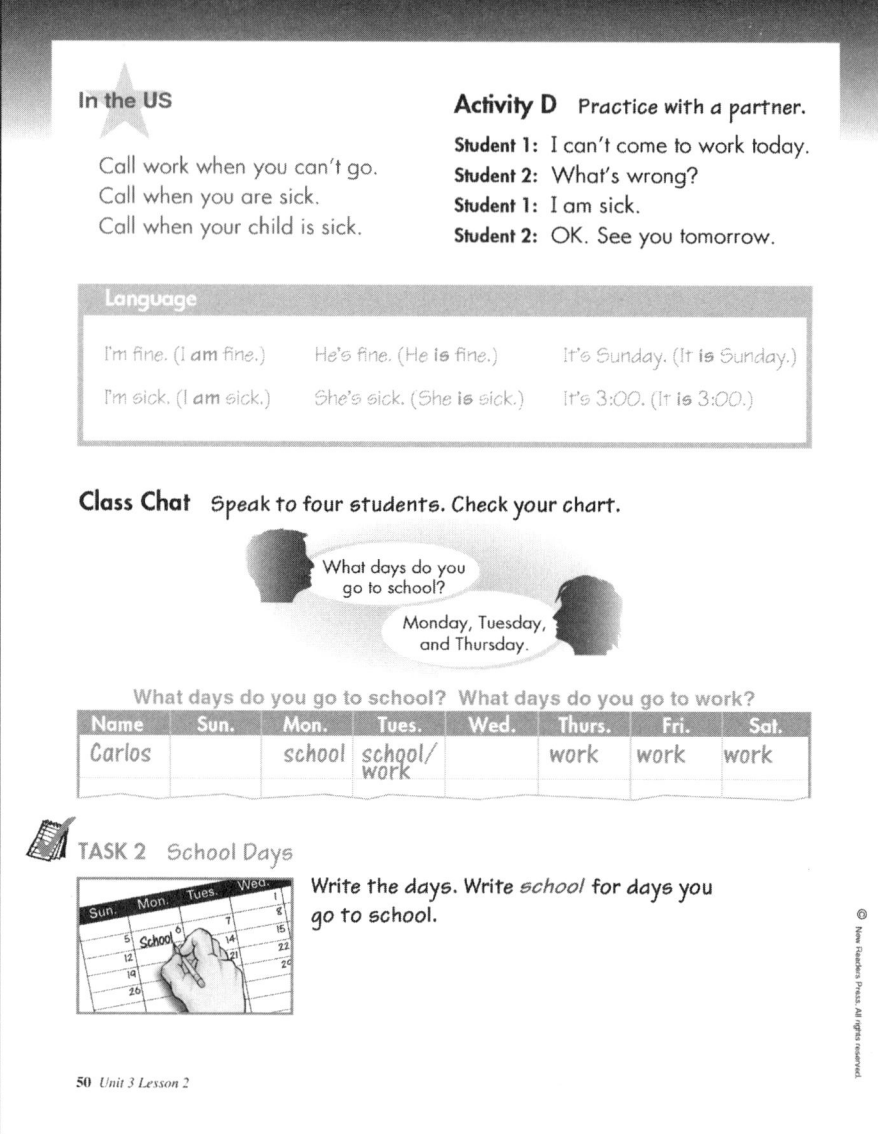

Task 2

Before learners begin Task 2, do the following:
- Draw a large calendar of a month on the board.
- Ask learners to call out and spell the days of the week.
- After writing the days, show learners when you work by writing *work* on the appropriate days.
- If you also go to school, write *school* on the days you attend.

 Use Customizable Master 6 (Calendar). Copy and distribute the master.
- Have learners copy the information you wrote on the board or transparency onto their calendars.
- When they finish, have them compare calendars with a partner.

 Assign Workbook pp. 32–34.

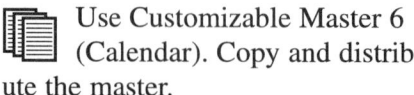 Use Unit Master 26 (Life Skills: Using Polite Language).

Cut out the lines of dialogue. Keep the lines of partners A and B in separate piles. Give one copy each of part A and part B to a pair of learners. Have them put the sentences in order.

Unit 3 Project

📄 Use Generic Assessment Masters 7 (Oral Communication Rubric) and 8 (Written Communication Rubric) to evaluate learner performance on the Unit 3 Project.

Learners will prepare a schedule of their weekly activities.

Get Ready

📄 Duplicate and distribute Unit Master 27 (Unit 3 Project: Your Week).

Do the Work

- Discuss weekly activities together. Write the words you elicit on the board or an overhead transparency.
- Have learners look at the examples on p. 51 in their books to see if there are any activities they have missed.
- Encourage them to write as many activities for the week as they can think of. Make sure they understand that they are not just writing words on the lines, but that the words should represent activities they are actually doing during the week.

Present Your Project

- Have learners work in groups of four, passing around their weekly schedules and showing them to group members.
- Encourage discussion of the activities.

Writing

Learners can now use the information from their Unit Project to write sentences about themselves. Circulate to help them generate these sentences.

Technology Extra

If learners have access to computers, have them use a word-processing program or a business card-making program to create a calendar for the current week. Have learners print out the calendar.

UNIT 3 Project

Your Week

Get Ready
Get a weekly calendar page.

Do the Work
Write your activities for the week. (examples: school, work, child's school, exercise)

Present Your Project
Show your calendar in class. Talk about your activities for the week.

Monday:	work, school
Tuesday:	work, exercise
Wednesday:	daughter's school, my school
Thursday:	work, exercise
Friday:	school
Saturday/Sunday:	mother's house

Writing
Write three sentences about your week.

work   exercise   stay home   go to school

On _____ I _____ .
    day of the week   what you do

On _____ I _____ .
    day of the week   what you do

On _____ I _____ .
    day of the week   what you do

Technology Extra
Find a calendar form on the computer.
Type your week's activities in the calendar.

One Step Up
Have learners who can type enter their sentences from the writing step of the Unit Project into a word-processing program.

📖 Assign Workbook p. 35 (Check Your Progress).

📄 Use Unit Master 28 (Unit 3 Checkup/Review) after you complete this unit.

Unit 4: Money, Money, Money!

Materials for the Unit
- Money—bills and change
- Play money
- Index cards
- Sample paychecks
- Calendar
- Sticky notes
- Copies of blank checks (optional)
- A variety of picture IDs (state license, driver's license, student ID, passport, consular ID, etc.)
- Calculators
- Card stock
- Game markers
- Unit Masters 29–35
- Customizable Masters 1–3
- Vocabulary Card Masters for Unit 4

Money, Money, Money!

Follow these steps to discuss the unit title:
- Display some money. If possible, include several one-dollar bills as well as a five, a ten, a twenty, and some coins.
- Ask learners, "What's this?"
- Count the paper money and say *bills*.
- Count the coins and say *change*.
- Ask learners to raise their hands if they have any bills or coins.
- Write on the board *bills/change = money*.

Photo

Follow the suggestions on p. 5 for talking about the photo.
Read the question below the arrow aloud and ask these *either/or* questions:
- Is this a man or a woman?
- Is she at home or at work?
- Is this a watch or a clock?
- Is she holding pens or envelopes?
- Is this a man or a woman?
- Is he opening a book or an envelope?
- Is he happy or sad?
- Is this a paycheck or a bill?

Caption

Read the caption aloud several times and have the learners repeat it.
- Ask learners who work to raise their hands.
- Start learners talking about paydays by asking the ones who work, "When is your payday?"
- Talk about your own payday.

Attention Box

Write the words from the word box on the board *(paycheck, payday)*.
- Point to your paycheck and say *paycheck*.
- Point to your payday on the calendar and say *payday*.

Picture Dictionary

Follow the suggestions on p. 6 for introducing vocabulary.

Follow the suggestions on p. 6 for using vocabulary cards. Use the Vocabulary Card Masters for the words in the Picture Dictionary.

Activity A

Remind learners of the meaning of *circle*.
- Write *bill* and *cash* on the board.
- Say, "Circle cash." Then circle the word *cash*.

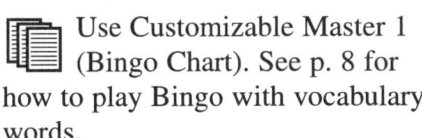 Play the audio or read the listening script below and have learners circle what they hear.

Encourage learners to use clarification language such as *please repeat* if they want to hear an item again.

Circulate to check learners' answers before reviewing the correct answers.

<u>Listening Script</u>
Listen. Circle.
1. coin
2. change
3. money order
4. amount
5. sign
6. cash

Use Customizable Master 1 (Bingo Chart). See p. 8 for how to play Bingo with vocabulary words.

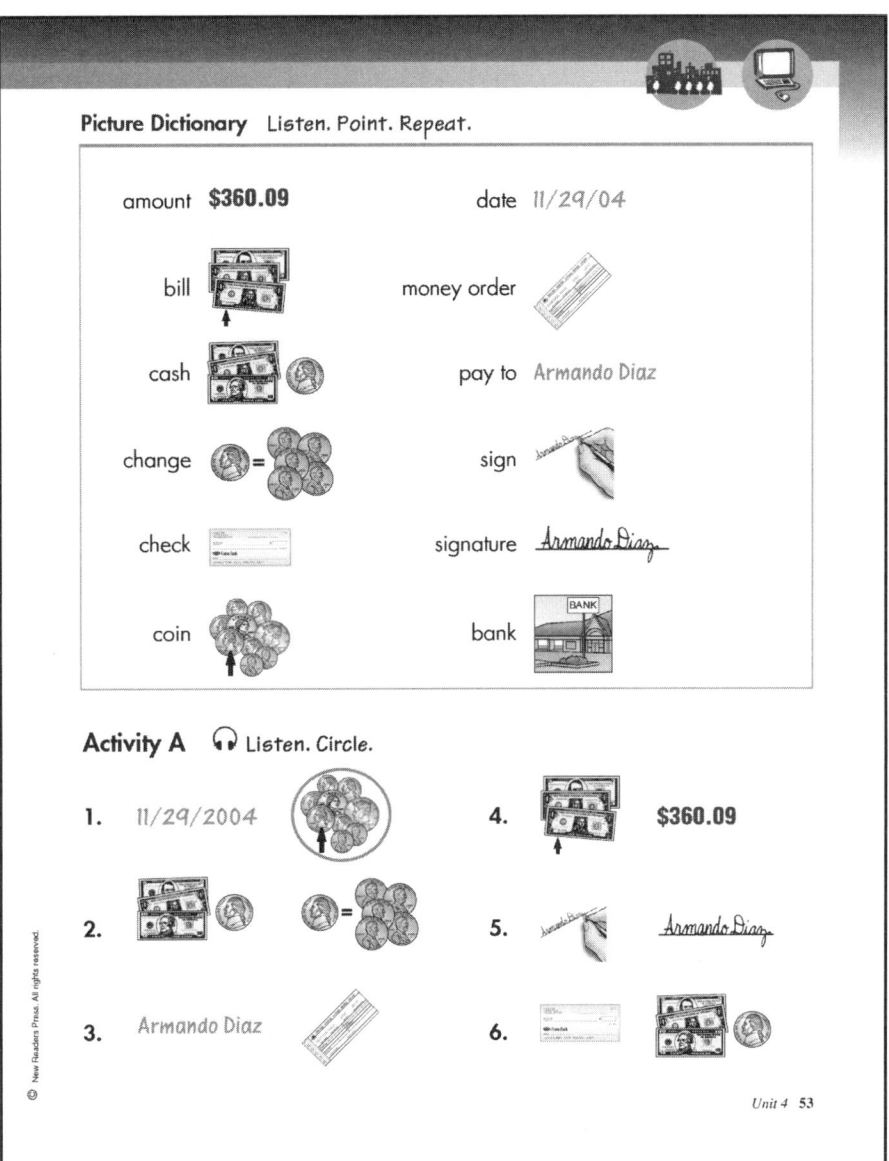

Lesson 1: At the Bank

Photos

Follow the suggestions on p. 5 for talking about the photo. Ask learners these *either/or* questions:

Photo 1
- Does Armando want money or food?
- Does he want one dollar or a hundred dollars?

Photo 2
- Is Armando sitting or standing?
- Is he in line or at the teller's window?

Photo 3
- Is Armando at work or at a bank?
- Is this Armando or a bank teller?
- Are these coins or bills?

Photo 4
- Does the teller or Armando speak?
- Does Armando say "Bye" or "Thanks"?

Point to the speech or thought bubble on each photo and have learners repeat the words aloud several times.

Comprehension

Have learners circle the correct answers.

Answers
1. no 2. yes 3. no
4. no 5. yes

Extension

After learners correct their answers, have them do the following:
- Read the story aloud in the correct order.
- Copy the sentences into their notebooks.
- Practice the conversation with a partner.

Ask for role-play volunteers to act out the story.

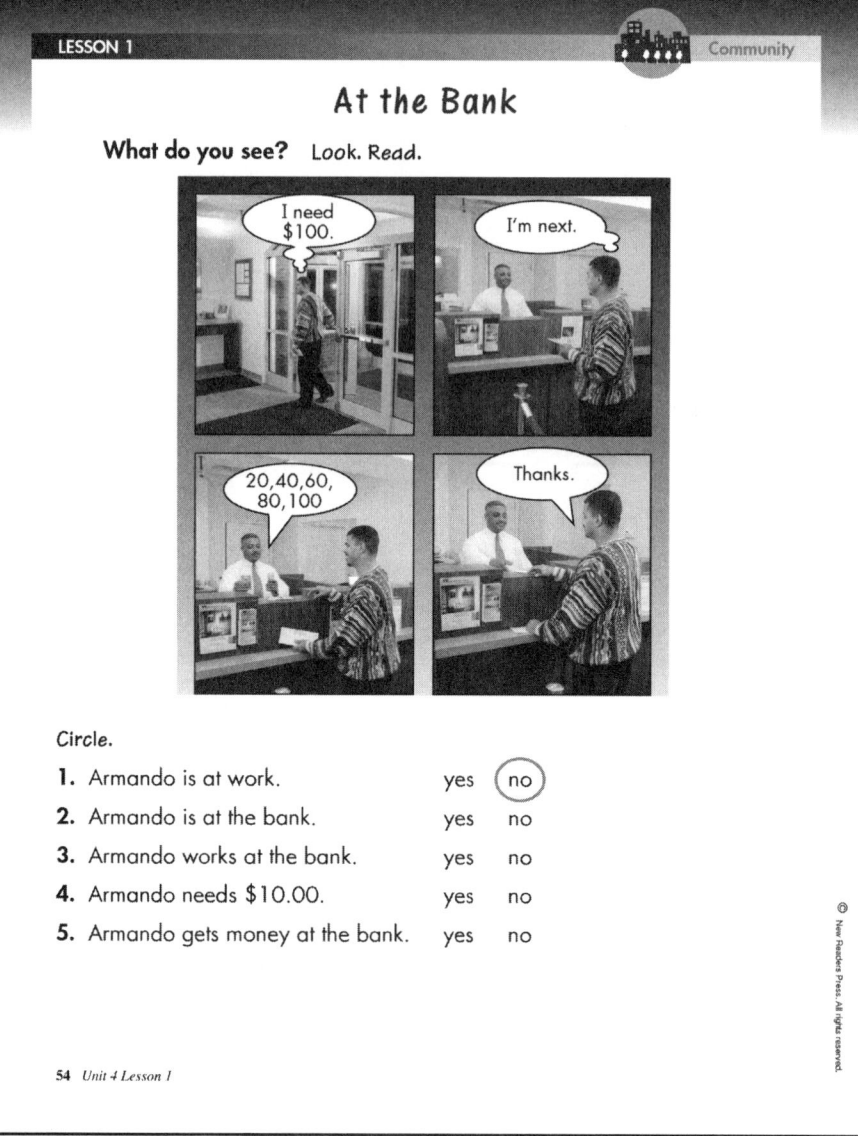

54 Unit 4 *Lesson 1*

Picture Dictionary

Follow the suggestions on p. 6 for introducing vocabulary.

Follow the suggestions on p. 6 for using vocabulary cards. Use the Vocabulary Card Masters for the words in the Picture Dictionary.

Have learners do the following matching activity:
- Pass out play money. Make sure each learner has a complete set of all denominations of bills and coins.
- Have learners match the play money with the correct words on the vocabulary cards.

After completing the activity, collect the play money and pass it out again. This time, make the activity more challenging by giving some learners incomplete sets of play money. Have them ask you or other learners for the bills they need to complete their sets (e.g., "I need $5.00.").

Class Chat

Use Customizable Master 3 (3-Column Chart). Follow the suggestions on p. 7 (Preparing for a Class Chat) for customizing and duplicating the master and distributing the copies.

Follow the suggestions on p. 7 for facilitating Class Chats.
- Give learners play money in several denominations. Some learners should have $20 bills but no $1 bills. Others should have $1, $5, or $10 bills, but no $20 bills.
- To make the Class Chat more challenging, change the headings in the chart, using coins.

Extension
Have learners write sentences using information from the chats. Then have them read their sentences to a partner.

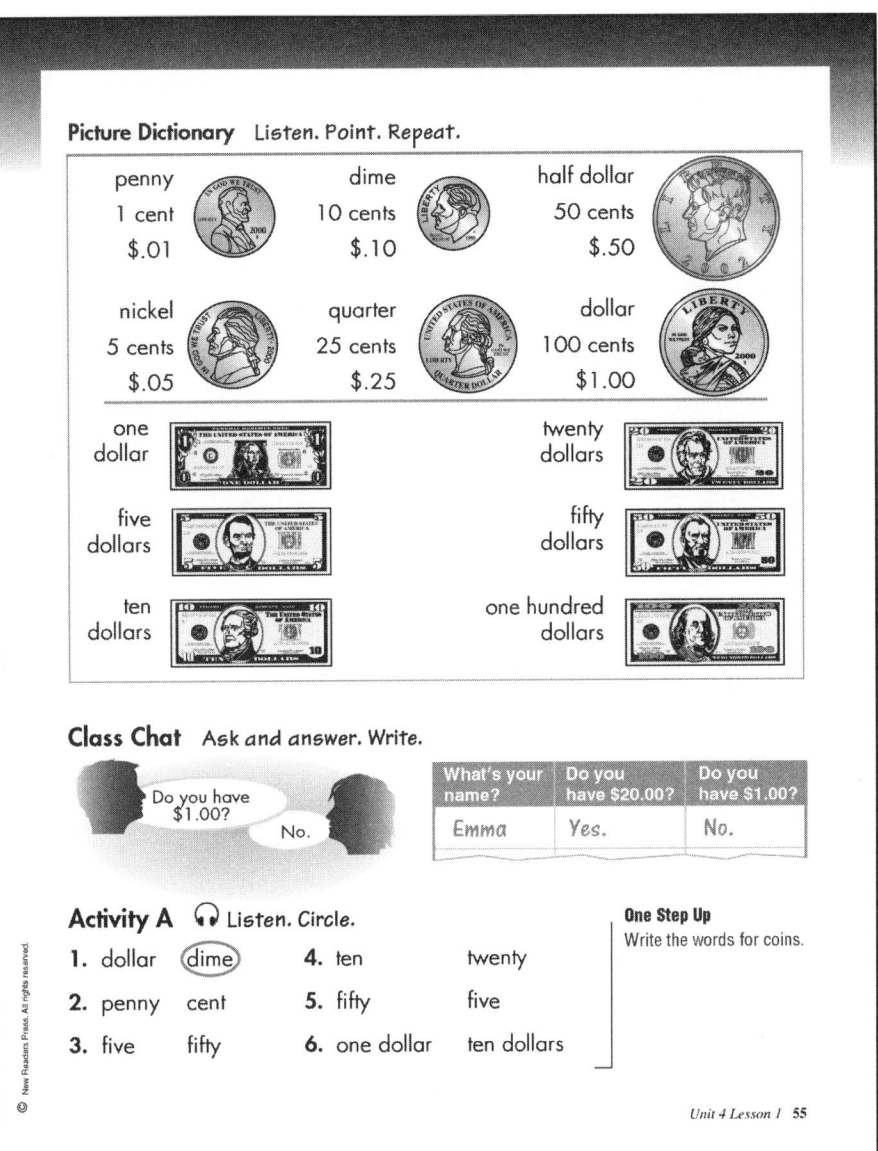

Activity A

Play the audio or read the listening script below. Have learners circle the words they hear.

Listening Script/Answers
Listen. Circle.
1. dime   4. ten
2. penny   5. five
3. fifty   6. one dollar

Extension
To provide additional practice in both comprehension and writing, dictate the spelling of five to seven words from the Picture Dictionary.

Unit 4 Lesson 1   55

Vocabulary

Follow the suggestions on p. 6 for introducing vocabulary.

Follow the suggestions on p. 6 for using vocabulary cards. Use the Vocabulary Card Masters for the words in the Vocabulary box.
- Read the numbers in order. Have learners hold up a vocabulary card for each number they hear.
- Say the numbers randomly as learners hold up their cards.
- Have learners do the same thing with a partner.
- Ask learners to scramble their cards, exchange them with a partner, and re-order them.

Activity B

Play the audio or read the listening script below. Have learners write the numbers.

Listening Script/Answers
Listen. Write numbers.
a. 85   c. 61   e. 97   g. 72
b. 70   d. 90   f. 60   h. 80

Activity C

Play the audio or read the listening script below. Have learners write the numbers in words.

Listening Script/Answers
Listen. Write words.
a. sixty-one   e. eighty-five
b. seventy-two   f. eighty
c. ninety   g. sixty
d. seventy   h. ninety-seven

Task 1

Model the activity by counting some real money. Then have learners count the money in the picture and write the total. Write the amount in numerals and words on the board.

Answers
$28.64, twenty-eight dollars and sixty-four cents

Extension
For more practice, do the following:
- Make word cards with money amounts in words and numbers.

56 Unit 4 Lesson 1

Vocabulary Listen. Point. Repeat.

60	70	80	90	100
sixty	seventy	eighty	ninety	one hundred
61	72	85	97	
sixty-one	seventy-two	eighty-five	ninety-seven	

Remember?

10	20	30	40	50
ten	twenty	thirty	forty	fifty

Activity B Listen. Write numbers.
a. 85   c. ___   e. ___   g. ___
b. ___ d. ___   f. ___   h. ___

Activity C Listen. Write words.
a. sixty-one   d. _____   g. _____
b. _____   e. _____   h. _____
c. _____   f. _____

TASK 1 Counting Money

Count the money. Write the money in numbers. Write the money in words.

- Scramble the cards and give one to each learner.
- Have learners find their match by circulating and reading their amounts to other learners.

Use Unit Master 29 (Game: Spend! Spend! Spend!) at any time after learners complete this page and Workbook p. 38.
- Copy the game board onto card stock.
- Have learners sit in small groups. Give one game board to each group along with a coin.
- The object of the game is to "go shopping." Learners flip a coin to move a marker one space for heads, two spaces for tails. (Flip a coin to show *heads* and *tails*.)
- Give each player a marker and $100.00 in play money. Ask one learner per group to hold extra money (i.e., to be the "bank").
- Learners take turns flipping the coin and moving their markers. Then they follow the directions on the square where they land.
- The game ends when someone runs out of money; the person with the most money left wins.

Use Unit Master 30 (Reading: The Letter *T*) now or at any time during the rest of the unit.

Assign Workbook pp. 36–38.

Lesson 2: Armando's First Paycheck

Before using this page with learners, do the following:
- Make a large copy of a paycheck or draw a picture of a paycheck on easel paper or poster board. (An enlarged copy of an actual check may be made on a photocopier; just be sure to obscure the payee's name, Social Security number, and other personal information.)
- Make vocabulary cards of the words in the comprehension activity.
- After the listening activity, give vocabulary cards to learners and have them tape the cards in the appropriate places on the enlarged paycheck.

Paycheck

Play the audio or read the listening script below several times. Have learners point to the numbers as they listen.

Listening Script
What do you see?
Look. Listen. Point. Repeat.
One. CBA Company—company name
Two. 08/06/04—date
Three. $360.09—amount in numbers
Four. Three hundred sixty dollars and nine cents—amount in words
Five. Armando Diaz—pay to
Six. Signature—James A. Curran

Comprehension

Have learners match each word in the column on the left with the corresponding item on the right.

Answers
1. e   3. b   5. a
2. d   4. c   6. f

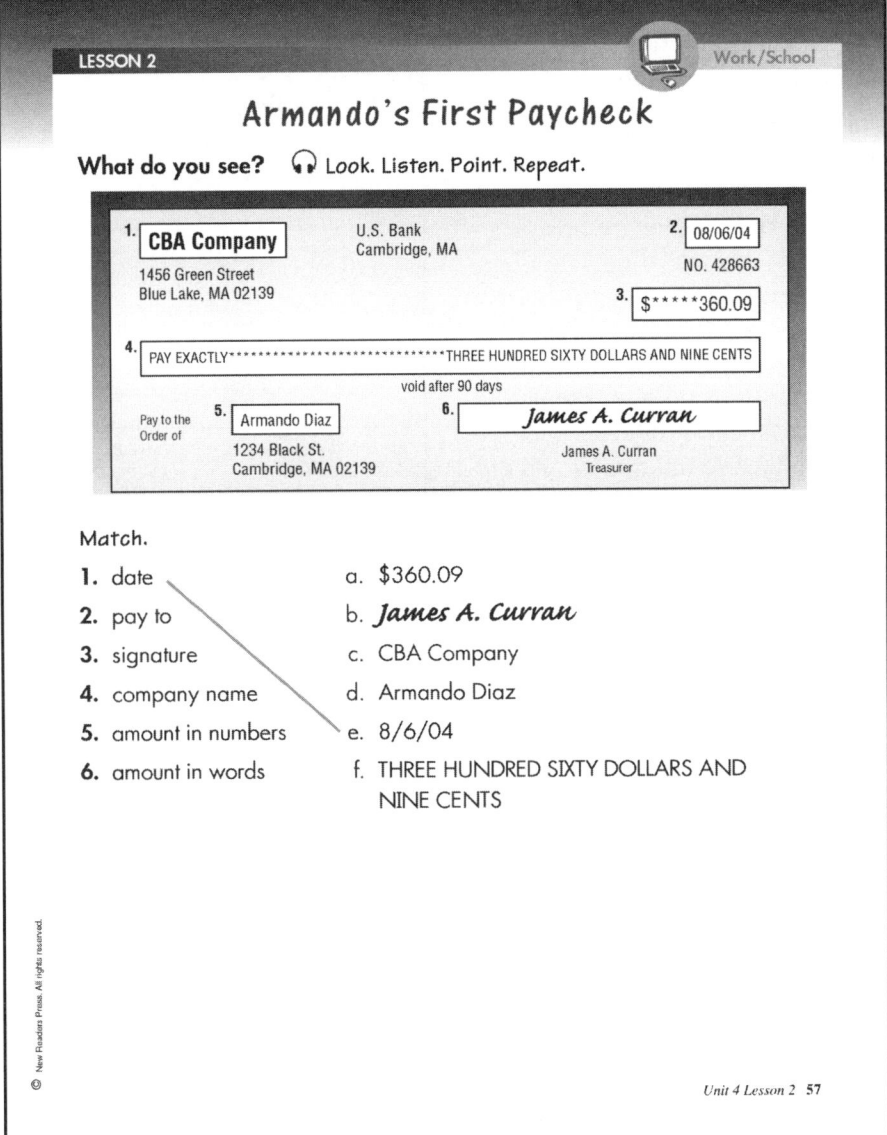

Unit 4 *Lesson 2* 57

Vocabulary

Follow the suggestions on p. 6 for introducing vocabulary.

Follow the suggestions on p. 6 for using vocabulary cards. Use the Vocabulary Card Masters for the words in the Vocabulary box.

Class Chat

Use Customizable Master 2 (2-Column Chart). Follow the suggestions on p. 7 (Preparing for a Class Chat) for customizing and duplicating the master and distributing copies.

Follow the suggestions on p. 7 for facilitating Class Chats.

Class Chat Follow-Up

Have learners write sentences based on the chats. Then have learners read their sentences to a partner, a small group, or the whole group.

Extension

Have learners line up according to their birthdays—month and day only. As a variation, write the names of the months on the board and have learners tell who has a birthday in each month.

In the US

Show learners the way dates are written in the US by using month, day, and year.

Activity A

As learners complete the writing task, circulate to monitor their work. If some learners need additional practice, make vocabulary cards of dates in words and numbers (e.g., *November 11, 2003*) and also in numbers alone (e.g., *11/11/03*) for a matching activity.

One Step Up

From this session forward, start every class by asking learners the day and date.

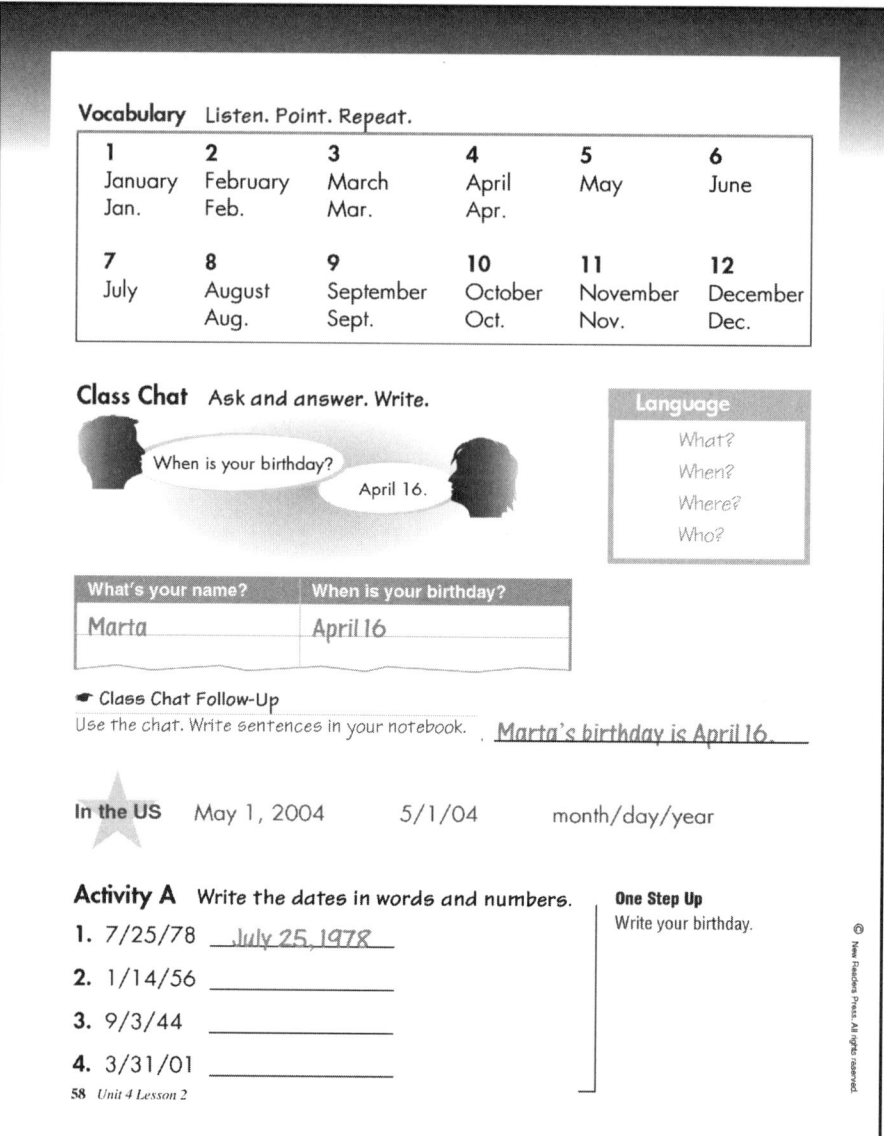

- Write the date in both numbers and words on the board or an overhead transparency.
- Explain the difference between *birth date* or *date of birth* and *birthday*. Explain that birth date always includes a year, but when we tell our birthdays, we only give the month and day.

Use Unit Master 31 (Reading: Months) now or at any time during the rest of the unit.

Have learners cut out the cards and, in groups of two or three, arrange the letters to spell names of months.

Demonstrate how to unscramble letters to make "real" English words:

- Use small sticky notes.
- Write one letter on each note.
- Put the notes on the board.
- Move the letters around until you have a word.

If learners seem ready, turn this activity into a game: Have teams compete with one another to see which will be first to unscramble the letters and make the names of all the months.

58 Unit 4 *Lesson 2*

Photo

Talk about the photo using the sentences below. Have learners point to items and people in the photo as you talk about them.
- Armando is at the supermarket.
- He is in a checkout line.
- He is holding a checkbook.
- The cashier says, "That's $93.67, please."
- Armando says, "OK."
- He writes a check.

Ask questions about the photo:
- Who is this?
- Where is he?
- What is he doing?
- What is he buying?
- How much is it?
- Does he pay cash?

Activity B

Before doing this activity, draw a large picture of a blank check on the board. Make vocabulary cards of the items learners will write on the check.

After learners write the check, review by distributing the vocabulary cards and having learners tape them in the correct places on the drawing.

<u>Extension</u>
Use a photocopier to prepare a page with facsimiles of several blank checks. Be sure all personal information such as account numbers has been removed. Provide information so learners can write the checks.

<u>One Step Up</u>
Legal documents require a signature. Some learners may know only how to print their names. Give learners who are interested a cursive model of their name to copy and practice. Do not be concerned about the signatures being in your writing style. Learners will adapt and personalize them.

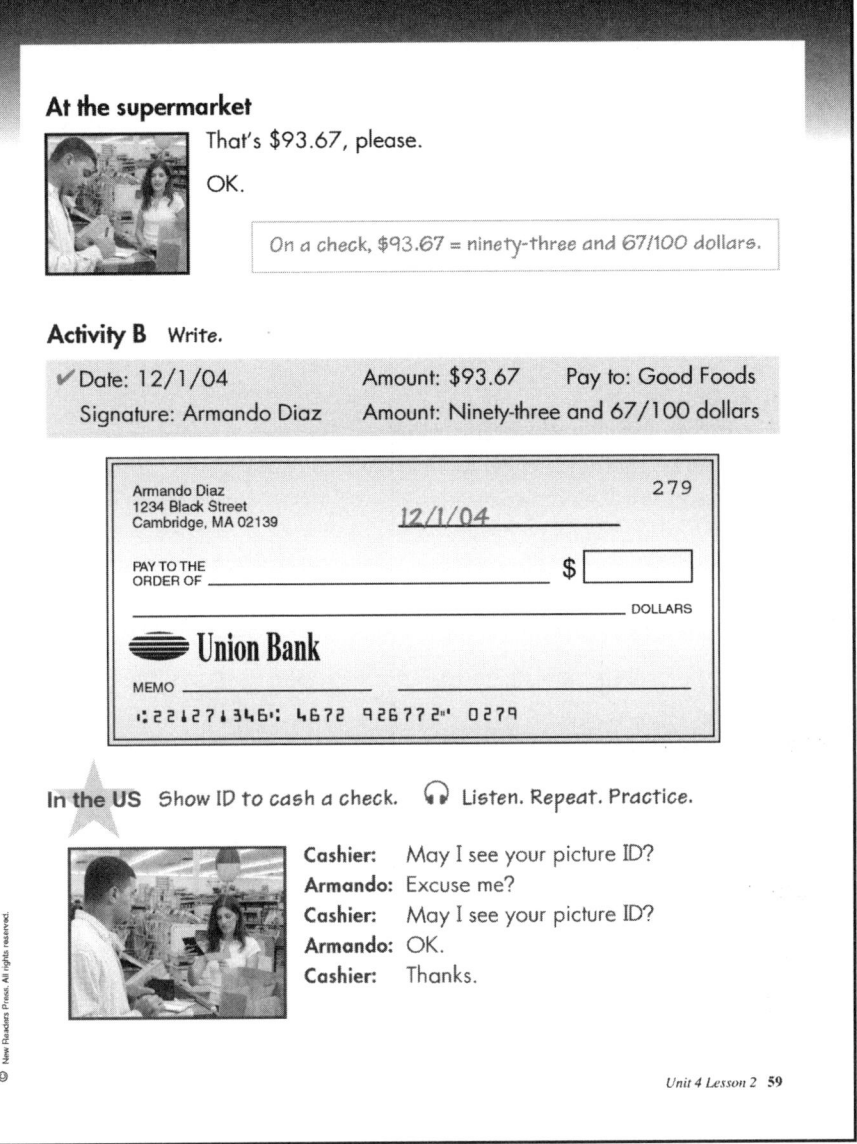

In the US

Play the audio or read the listening script below while learners follow along.

Have learners take turns role-playing the conversation for the class.

Show learners a variety of picture IDs and ask them to raise their hands for each type they have.

<u>Listening Script</u>
Listen. Repeat. Practice.
Cashier: May I see your picture ID?
Armando: Excuse me?
Cashier: May I see your picture ID?
Armando: OK.
Cashier: Thanks.

Use Unit Master 32 (Life Skills: Writing a Check) now or at any time during the rest of the unit.

Unit 4 *Lesson* 2 59

Picture Dictionary

Follow the suggestions on p. 6 for introducing vocabulary.

Follow the suggestions on p. 6 for using vocabulary cards. Use the Vocabulary Card Masters for the words in the Picture Dictionary.

Activity C

- While learners write the names of the places pictured, circulate to monitor their work.
- Review the answers with them.
- Ask individual learners to go to the board and write each answer.
- Have learners practice spelling the words for places in the community.

<u>Answers</u>
1. post office   5. hospital
2. gas station   6. pharmacy
3. restaurant   7. currency exchange
4. laundromat 8. supermarket

Task 2

Have learners write sentences about the method of payment they use at various places. Provide a model for them to follow (e.g., "I pay cash at the video store."). Have learners read their sentences to a partner, a small group, or the whole group.

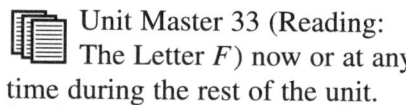 Unit Master 33 (Reading: The Letter *F*) now or at any time during the rest of the unit.

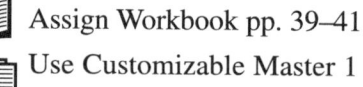 Assign Workbook pp. 39–41.

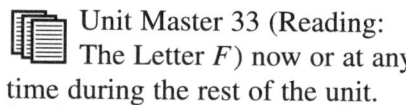 Use Customizable Master 1 (Bingo Chart). See p. 8 for how to play Vocabulary Bingo.

<u>Extension</u>

 Play Concentration with vocabulary cards to review vocabulary. Use the Vocabulary Card Masters for the words introduced on pp. 53, 55, 56, 58, and 60. See directions for the game on p. 9.

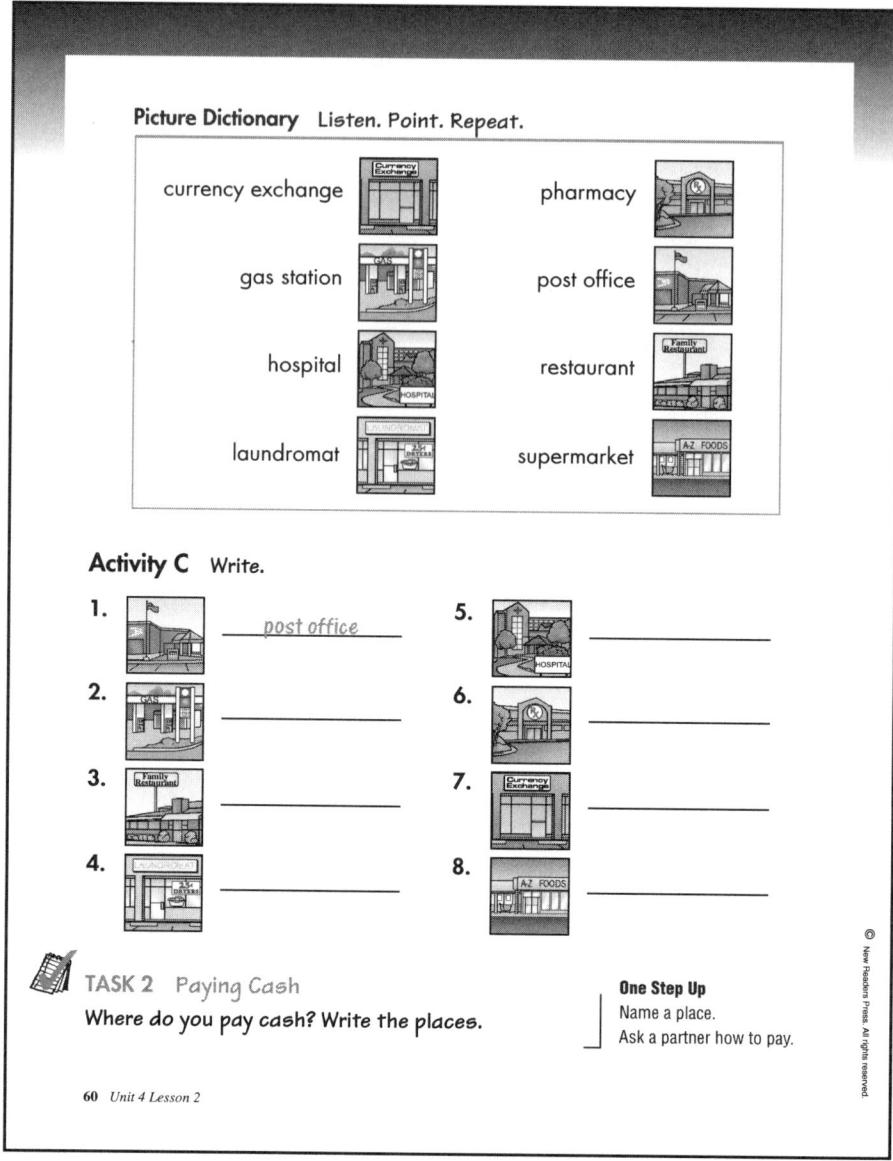

60 Unit 4 *Lesson 2*

Unit 4 Project

Learners use the vocabulary and skills from the unit to make a list of places where they pay cash.

Get Ready

- Have learners sit in groups of four. Assign a recorder, reporter, timekeeper, and materials leader in each group.
- Ask the timekeepers to record starting and ending times for each stage of their group's project.
- Prepare copies of Unit Master 34 (Unit 4 Project). Distribute the copies to the materials leaders along with scissors so they can cut out the copies.
- Review the names of the places pictured at the top of p. 61.
- Ask learners to write in their notebooks the names of two more places where they spend money. Help with spelling.

Do the Work

Ask learners to use the information from Task 2 to make a group list of places where they pay using cash. Have each group's writer prepare the group list.

Present Your Project

- Have the reporter in each group read the group list to the class.
- Use the group lists to assemble a class list on the board. Place tally marks after any entry mentioned by more than one group.

<u>One Step Up</u>

Make sentences about the information and have learners repeat them (e.g., "Learners in this class pay cash at the supermarket.").

Then count together how many people pay cash at each place (e.g., "Twelve students pay cash at the supermarket.").

Technology Extra

- Ask learners to bring calculators from home or use class sets if you have them.

UNIT 4 Project

Places You Pay Cash

Get Ready
Get into a group of four.

Do the Work
Use Task 2 on page 60. Where do you pay cash? Write a group list of places.

Present Your Project
Read your list to the class. Make a class list of places.

Technology Extra
Use a calculator. Write numbers.

Add: $40 + 55 + 79 =$ _____
Subtract: $100 - 38 =$ _____
Multiply: $67 \times 85 =$ _____
Divide: $100 \div 4 =$ _____

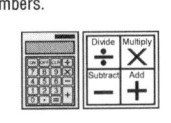

One Step Up
Use a calculator. Write the amounts.

2 quarters + 3 dimes + 4 pennies = _____

4 twenties + 3 fives + 7 ones = _____

Unit 4 Project 61

- Draw a large diagram of a calculator on the board or an overhead transparency.
- Point out the number keys and the four function keys.
- Show learners how to enter numbers and perform calculations.
- Have learners solve the problems individually or in pairs.

Answers
$40 + 55 + 79 = 174$
$100 - 38 = 62$
$67 \times 85 = 5,695$
$100 \div 4 = 25$

One Step Up

If learners enjoy solving equations using calculators, provide them with additional equations to solve. As a variation, give learners index cards and have them write problems. Collect the cards and redistribute them to the learners to solve.

Answers

2 quarters + 3 dimes + 4 pennies = 84 cents

4 twenties + 3 fives + 7 ones = $102

 Assign Workbook p. 42, Check Your Progress.

Use Unit Master 35 (Unit 4 Checkup/Review) when you complete this unit.

Unit 5: No Milk

Materials for the Unit
- Sticky notes
- Play money (particularly bills)
- Receipts from supermarkets
- Empty cans or cartons from common food items
- Bowl, spoon, common food items
- Sack of potatoes
- Scale or small hand weight
- Full-page supermarket ads from newspapers
- Unit Masters 36–41
- Customizable Masters 1–2
- Vocabulary Card Masters for Unit 5

No Milk
Follow these steps to discuss the unit title:
- Write the word *milk* on the board in large letters and draw a gallon of milk next to it. Color in the gallon so that it looks full. Point to it and say *milk*.
- Slowly erase the contents so that it appears the milk is gone.
- Now say *no milk*.
- Have learners say *no milk* several times.

Photo
Follow the suggestions on p. 5 for talking about the photo.

Read the question below the arrow aloud and ask these *either/or* questions:
- Is this a home or a school?
- Are there two people or three?
- Is this the father or the mother?
- Are there two women or two children?
- Are the people happy or sad? (Use facial prompts as you ask this question.)
- What are the children doing? Are they eating or playing?

Caption
- Read the photo caption aloud several times and have learners repeat.

- Ask, "Is there milk?" and "Do they need milk?" Then ask learners what they think the unit will be about.

Class Story
Follow the suggestions on p. 8 for writing class stories using a photo.

62 Unit 5

Picture Dictionary

If possible, bring in the following items to demonstrate the words: bowl, spoon, cereal, milk.

Follow the suggestions on p. 6 for introducing vocabulary.

Follow the suggestions on p. 6 for using vocabulary cards. Use the Vocabulary Card Masters for the words in the Picture Dictionary.

Hold up the vocabulary cards or items and ask *either/or* questions like these:
- Is this a bowl or a spoon?
- Is this a table or a refrigerator?
- Is this milk or cereal?

Activity A

Have learners write the words and then copy them into their notebooks.
- Circulate to monitor learners' work.
- Point to the words randomly and ask learners to say them.
- Point to the words randomly and ask learners to spell them.

Answers
1. refrigerator
2. table
3. children
4. spoon
5. morning
6. bowl
7. cereal
8. milk
9. kitchen
10. breakfast

Extensions
1. Have learners work in pairs using their vocabulary cards. One learner shows a card and the other says the word.
2. Have learners dictate the words to each other.
3. Have learners write the words in alphabetical order in their notebooks. Then have the class come to the board one by one to write the words alphabetically on the board.
4. To practice spelling, one partner can ask, "How do you spell _____?" The other partner spells the word. Circulate to monitor the pair practice.

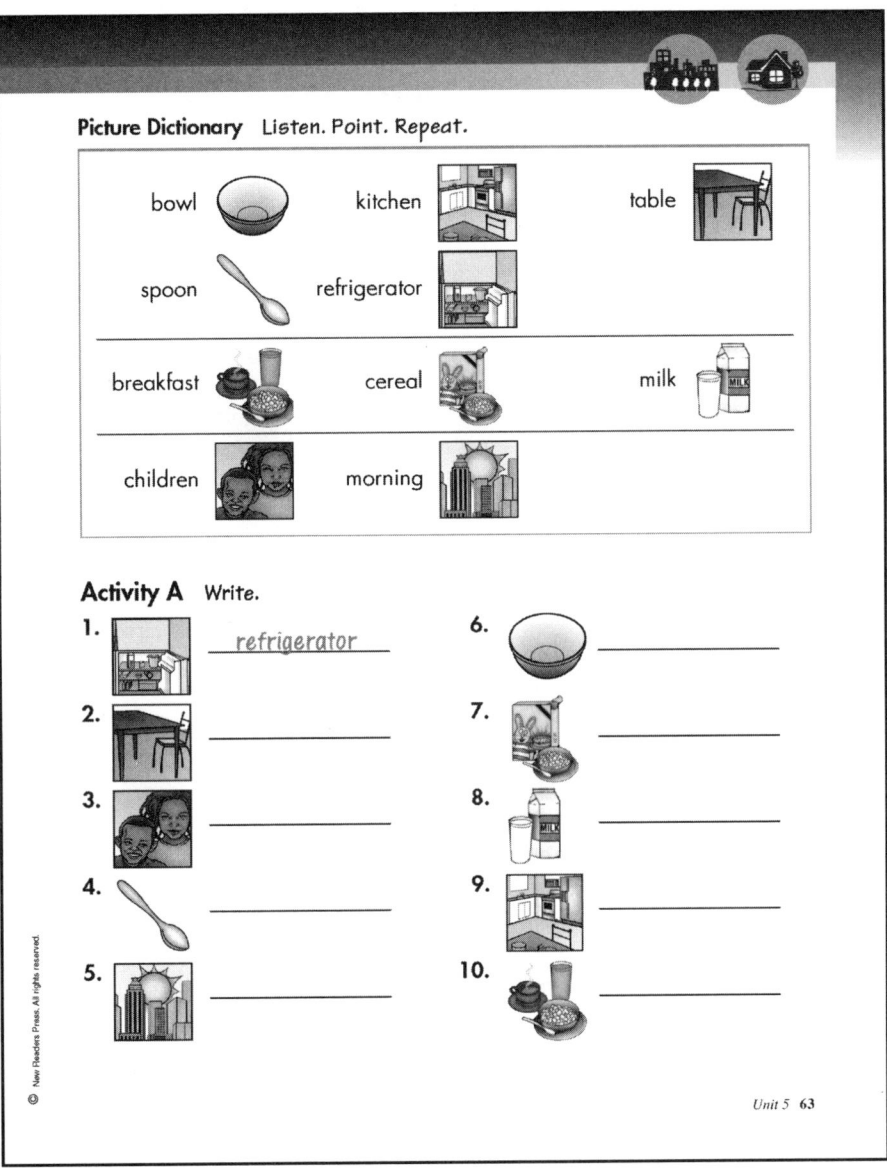

Unit 5 63

Lesson 1: Grocery Shopping

Photo

Follow the suggestions on p. 5 for talking about photos.

Ask learners, "What do you see?" Then ask these questions:
- Where is the family?
- What food do you see?
- What do they need?
- Read the caption several times and have learners repeat it.

Listening

 Play the audio or read the listening script below.

After learners listen, ask again any of the questions above that they had difficulty with.

Listening Script
Look. Listen. Point.
Greg and his wife, Ann, are at the supermarket. Their children are with them. They are in the dairy section. The wife is buying milk. There are eggs, butter, and milk in this part of the supermarket.

Comprehension

Follow the suggestions on p. 6 for listening/reading comprehension.

Follow these steps:
- Play the audio or read the listening script below twice.
- Have learners point to the correct words as they listen.
- Have them listen a third time and circle the correct words.
- Play the audio or read the listening script again.
- Have learners check their work.
- Have them exchange books or papers to correct the work.
- Give them time to write the correct words in their notebooks.

Listening Script
Listen. Circle.
Milk.   Circle *milk*.   Milk.
Daughter. Circle *daughter*. Daughter.
Eggs.   Circle *eggs*.   Eggs.
Butter.   Circle *butter*.   Butter.

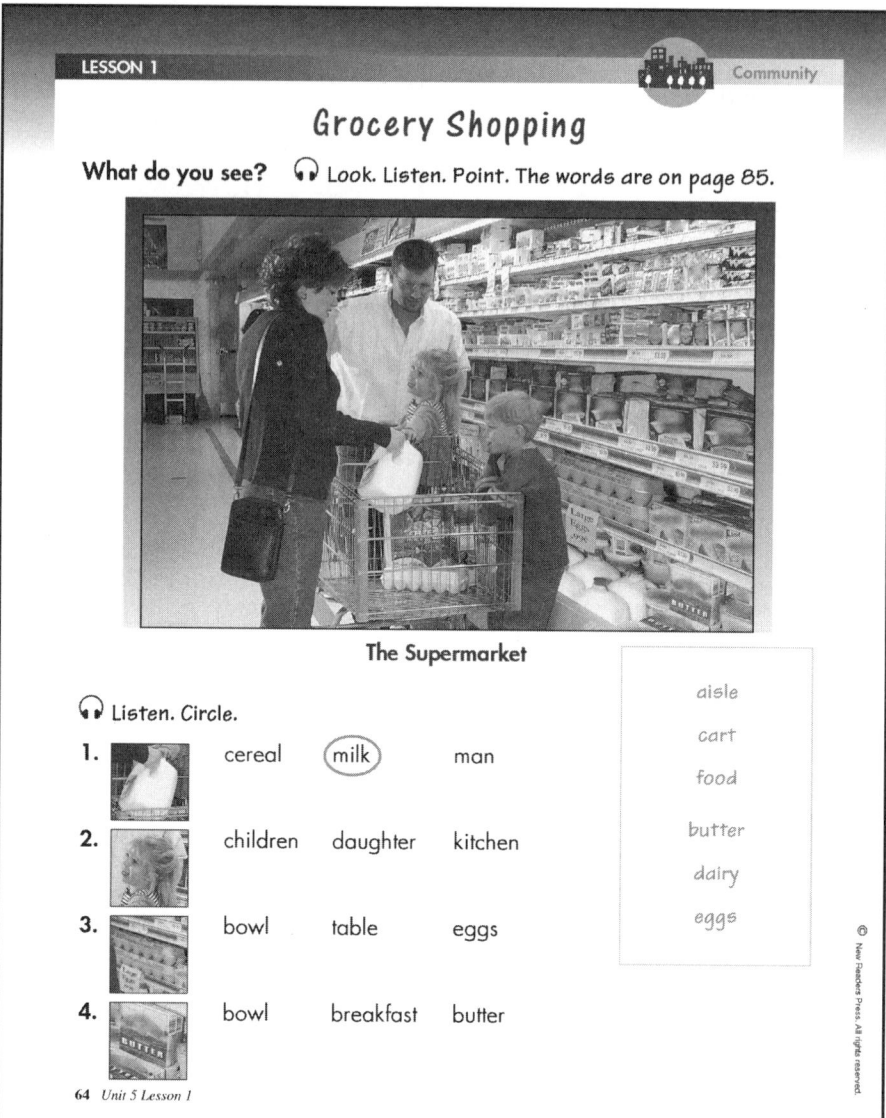

Answers
1. milk   3. eggs
2. daughter   4. butter

Extensions
1. Distribute vocabulary cards— one set to each group of three or four learners. Ask them to use the alphabet on p. 33 to alphabetize the new words.
2. Have learners dictate their lists to you as you write them on the board.
3. Have pairs of learners take turns dictating the new words to each other.

Picture Dictionary

If possible, bring in real food items to demonstrate the words.

Follow the suggestions on p. 6 for introducing vocabulary.

Follow the suggestions on p. 6 for using vocabulary cards. Use the Vocabulary Card Masters for the words in the Picture Dictionary.

Hold up the vocabulary cards or food items and ask *either/or* questions like these:
- Is this a tomato or a carrot?
- Is this beef or a banana?
- Is this fish or fruit?

Place vocabulary cards for the category words *meat, seafood, fruit,* and *vegetables* on a table.
- Pass out the other vocabulary cards and ask learners to place them under the correct category card so that they practice the skill of categorizing.
- Pass out vocabulary cards or sticky notes and have learners affix them to the items you have collected.

In the US

Show how weight is measured in pounds. If possible, have a sack of potatoes available—even an empty sack with clearly marked weight is fine. As an alternative, bring in a scale or a small hand weight (on these, the weight is usually written in both kilos and pounds). Since the United States is nearly alone in the world in the use of pounds, this measure will probably represent a new concept for learners.

Point out the abbreviation for *pound (lb./lbs.)*, which has no clear relationship with the word.

<u>One Step Up</u>
- Show that 16 ounces equal one pound.
- Show the abbreviation for *ounce*.
- Show the relationship between kilos and pounds: 1 kilo = 2.2 pounds.

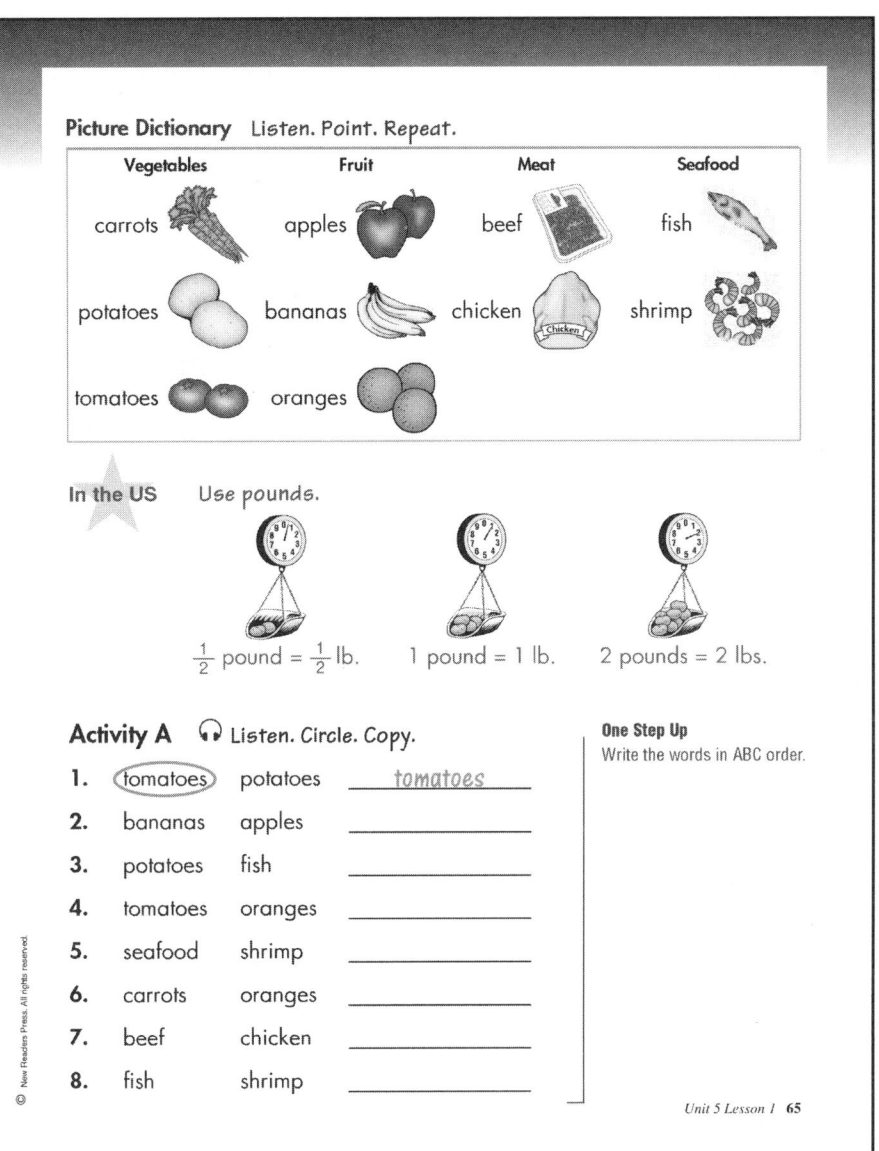

Activity A

Before learners do the activity, play the audio or read the listening script below as you point to the answers. Then follow these steps:
- Play the audio or read the listening script twice and have learners circle the words they hear.
- Have learners copy the words.
- Play the audio or read the words once more so learners can check their work.

<u>Listening Script/Answers</u>
Listen. Circle.
1. tomatoes   5. shrimp
2. apples   6. carrots
3. potatoes   7. beef
4. oranges   8. fish

Now copy the words.

Use Unit Master 36 (Life Skills: Organize Information). Make copies for learners. First lead them orally in the activity. Then have them complete it in writing.

Use Unit Master 37 (Reading: The Letter *H*) now or at any time during the rest of the unit.

Unit 5 *Lesson 1* 65

Picture Dictionary

Follow the suggestions on p. 6 for introducing vocabulary.

Follow the suggestions on p. 6 for using vocabulary cards. Use the Vocabulary Card Masters for the words in the Picture Dictionary.

Hold up the vocabulary cards and ask *either/or* questions like these:
- Is this bread or beans?
- Is this rice or noodles?
- Is this coffee or tea?

Pass out vocabulary cards and have learners tape them to the food items you have brought.

Activity B

Play the audio or read the listening script below. Have learners complete the activity orally before they write the words.
- Have them listen again and write which food items they hear. Stop the audio or pause as you read to give them time to write.
- Play the audio or read the listening script again so that learners can check their work.

Listening Script
Listen. Write.
a. Do you need coffee?
   Coffee?   Yes!
b. Do you like noodles?
   Noodles?   Yes!
c. Do you want tea?
   Tea?   Yes, please.
d. Do you need water?
   I'd love water!
e. Do you need oil?
   Oil?   Yes, please.
f. Do you like beans?
   Beans?   No!
g. Do you want more rice?
   Rice?   Yes, please.
h. Do you like bread?
   Bread?   Yes!
i. Do you need juice?
   Juice?   Yes, I do.

Answers
a. coffee   d. water   g. rice
b. noodles   e. oil   h. bread
c. tea   f. beans   i. juice

In the US

Explain the words *breakfast, lunch,* and *dinner* as meals eaten in the morning, afternoon, and evening.

Class Chat

Follow the suggestions on p. 7 for facilitating Class Chats.

Task 1

Before learners write, have them call out the names of the stores they frequent and their locations. Write these on the board. Compare learners' responses.
- How many learners shop at the same store?
- Do they like where they shop?
- Why or why not?

Extensions
1. On the board or an overhead transparency, tally how many learners shop at each store.
2. Ask questions about the stores:
   - Is it a good store?
   - Do you like to shop there?
   - Are prices good?

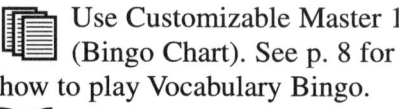
Use Customizable Master 1 (Bingo Chart). See p. 8 for how to play Vocabulary Bingo.

Assign Workbook pp. 43–45.

Lesson 2: A Shopping List

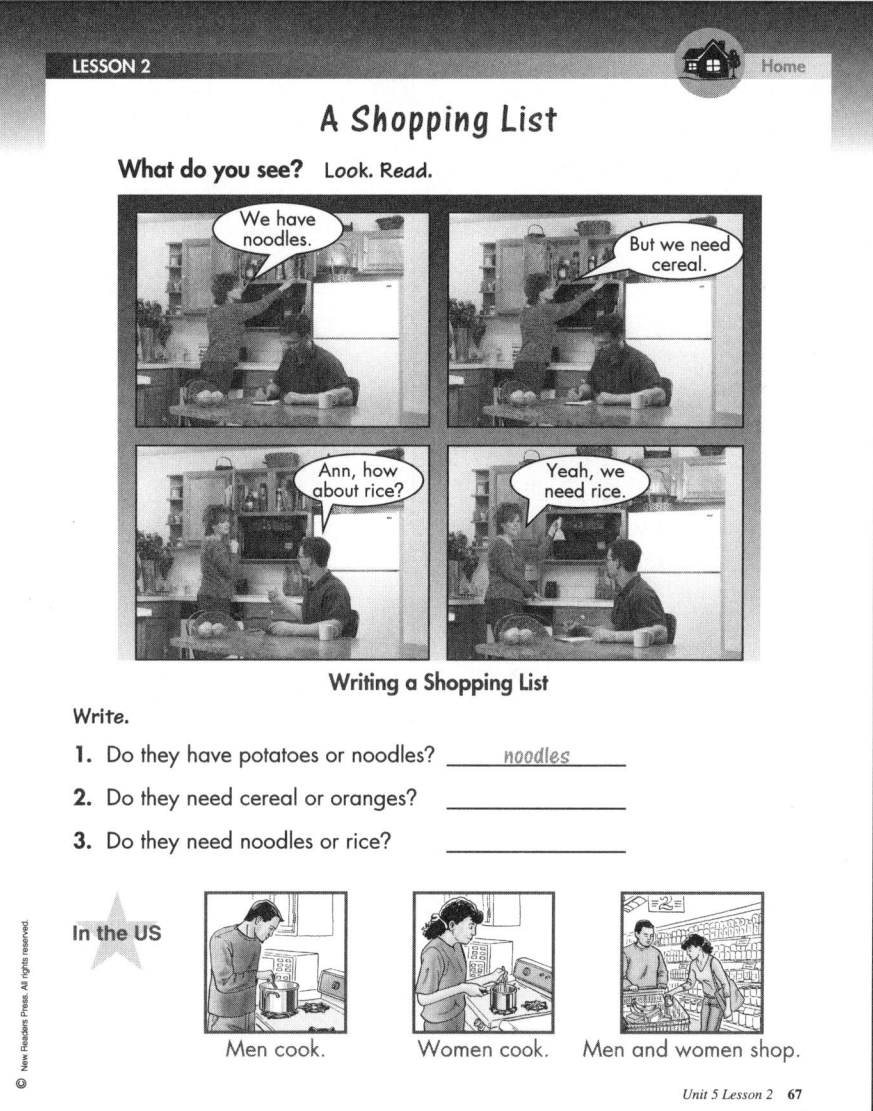

Photos

Read the caption and have learners repeat it several times.

Follow the suggestions on p. 5 for talking about photos. Point to the speech bubble in each photo frame and have learners repeat the words aloud several times. Then ask the following questions:

Photo 1
- Who is she?
- Where is she—in a store or at home?

Photo 2
- Does she have cereal?
- Does she need cereal?

Photo 3
- Who is he?
- Where is he?
- What is he doing?

Photo 4
- Does she have rice?
- Does she need rice?

Extensions
1. Have learners read the story in pairs.
2. Have some pairs perform the story for the class.

Writing

Learners should be able to read and write the answers to these questions independently. Circulate to monitor their work.

If learners are having problems with the writing activity, ask the questions orally and then have them write the answers.

Answers
1. noodles   2. cereal   3. rice

One Step Up
Ask what Ann and Greg need. After learners say the items, have them list the items in alphabetical order.

In the US

Ask learners these questions:
- Do you go to the supermarket?
- Do you shop with your family?
- Do men shop for food in the US? Do women?
- Do men shop for food in your home country? Do women?

Explain that in the United States, men *and* women shop for food for the family.

Use questions like those above to ask learners about cooking in the US and in their home countries.

Unit 5 *Lesson 2* 67

Vocabulary

Follow the suggestions on p. 6 for introducing vocabulary.

Follow the suggestions on p. 6 for using vocabulary cards. Use the Vocabulary Card Masters for the words in the Vocabulary box.

Present the concepts *more* and *less* introducing the vocabulary.
- Use cartons or sacks from the grocery items you have brought.
- Compare very differently sized items (e.g., gallon vs. pint).
- Tape the *more* card to a gallon and the *less* card to a pint.
- Reinforce the concept using two cartons or bags of cereal.

To present the math concepts *add* and *subtract*, use items that can be combined (e.g., apples, oranges, or bananas).
- Demonstrate combining *(add)* items and taking away *(subtract)* items. Write the corresponding problem (e.g., 3 apples + 2 apples = 5 apples) on the board or an overhead transparency.
- Pace your math problems according to your learners' abilities. If some learners are having obvious difficulty grasping the concepts, pair them with learners who know the material well.

Activity A

Read the activity together and have learners fill in the blanks orally. Then have them write the answers. Review the answers orally, either as a whole group or in smaller groups.

Answers
1. add   5. plus
2. subtract   6. minus
3. more   7. change
4. less

Extension
Provide supermarket receipts and follow these steps:
- Ask two learners to role-play the cashier and the shopper.

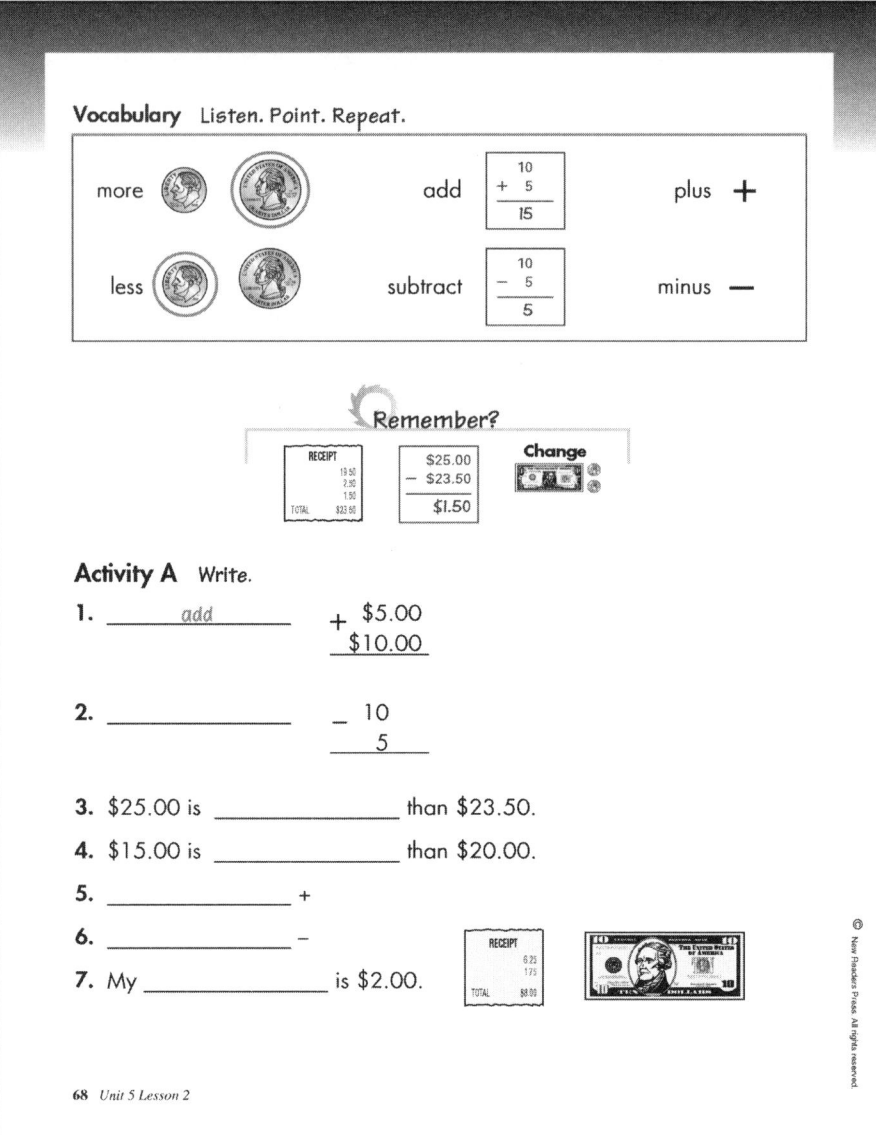

- Give the shopper play money bills and the cashier a receipt. The cashier says the total.
- The shopper gives the cashier money to pay for the items.
- Write the amount the shopper gives the cashier on the board. Ask the class to subtract the amount due from the total paid.
- The cashier states the change and the two say parting remarks.

Use Unit Master 38 (Game: Match the Facts) now or at any time during the rest of the unit.
- Have learners work in pairs.
- Cut out the amounts at the bottom of the page.

- Each pair gets a set of problems and a set of answers.
- One learner picks up an amount and reads it aloud. The pair then tries to find the problem that fits. The first pair to finish wins.

Activity B

Write the change amounts on the board so that learners are able to concentrate on listening and speaking.
- Choose two learners to read the speech bubbles aloud.
- Assign them the roles of Student A and Student B.
- Have them role-play a conversation based on the dollar amounts shown in the first row in the chart.
- Pair the other learners and ask them to complete the activity. Assist them as needed.

Answers
$.50
$1.01
$3.25
$4.55

Class Chat

Use Customizable Master 2 (2-Column Chart). Follow the suggestions on p. 7 (Preparing for a Class Chat) for customizing and duplicating the master and distributing the copies.

Follow the suggestions on p. 7 for facilitating Class Chats.
- Ask learners to circulate to collect the names of foods other learners need at home.
- Have them write learners' names and needed food items on their charts.

Class Chat Follow-Up
Make a list of common food items on the board.
- Ask questions about the foods (e.g., Who needs apples?).
- Under each question, write the names of learners who need that particular item.

Language

Focus on the introduction of the *do/don't* forms for the simple present tense. This is an opportunity to show the difference between *yes* and *no* answers in writing and in speech.

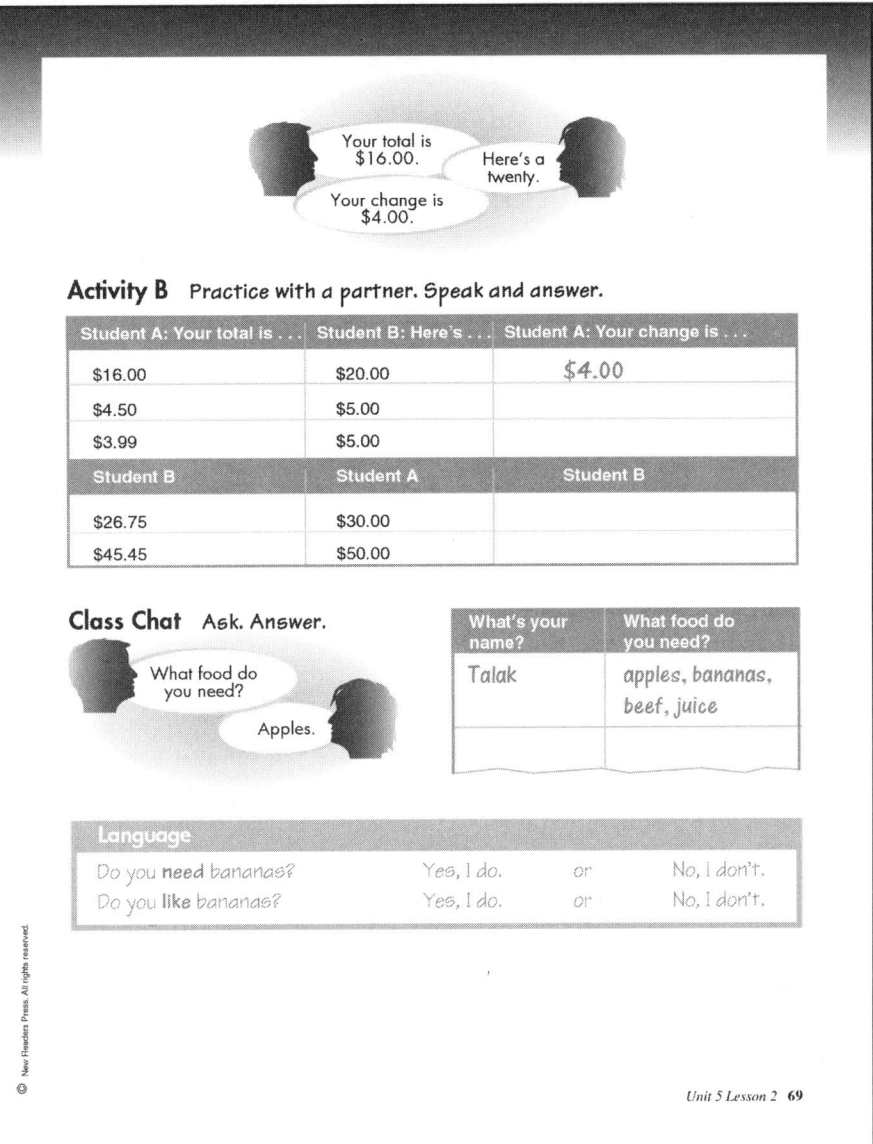

Have learners listen, point, and repeat as you read each column.
- Read the question twice, first following it with the positive answer and then with the negative one.
- Point out the difference in forming the dot over a lowercase *i* vs. the apostrophe in *don't*.
- Ask questions about likes and needs. Elicit full-sentence answers if possible, but be aware that learners have limited vocabulary.

Extension
Have learners work in pairs to ask and answer questions related to these forms.

In the US

Have some full-page supermarket ads available for this session. Pass the ads around for learners to see.

Ask questions like, "How much are _____?" and "Is that a good price?"

Explain that in the US, supermarkets offer sales on items. Good prices bring people to the store to shop. People can compare prices by looking at newspaper ads.

Ask learners if this happens in their home countries. Ask questions like, "Are there supermarket ads in newspapers?" and "Do you read prices in newspapers?"

Extension
- Ask groups of three or four learners to review the ads. Ask, "Are the prices good?" and "Is this more or less than you pay?"
- Ask the groups to read the ads aloud together and talk about them.

Activity C

Ask learners these questions:
- How much are the bananas on the left?
- How much are the bananas on the right?
- Which is more?
- Which is less?

Ask learners to read the answers modeled in the first picture pair. Then do the second pair together. Have learners do the third and fourth pairs independently.

Circulate to monitor learners' work.

Answers
2. more, less
3. more, less
4. less, more

Task 2

Help learners begin the task by asking these questions:
- Think about your kitchen at home.
- Think about the food in your kitchen.
- What foods do you need?

Tell learners to think about the food categories they have learned. Then do the following:
- Write the word *fruit* on the board. Ask a learner if he or she needs any fruit. If so, write the name of the fruit under the word *fruit* on the board. Continue until you have a few types of fruit.
- Follow the same procedure for listing vegetables, meat products, dairy products, and seafood.
- Ask for other food items that do not fit into the categories (e.g., salt, noodles, cereal).

After learners complete the task, have them look at each other's lists and read them aloud.

Use Unit Master 39 (Reading: The Letter *L*) now or at any time during the rest of the unit.

Assign Workbook pp. 46–48.

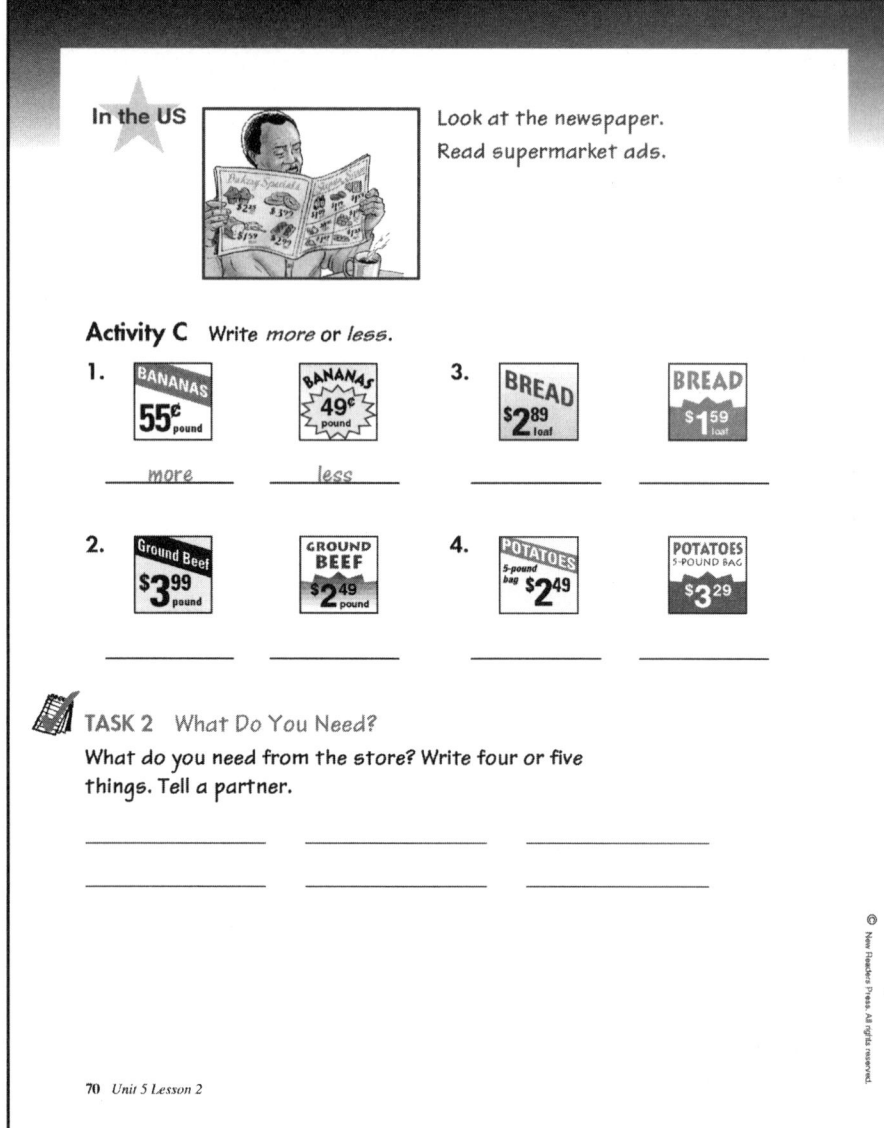

Unit 5 Project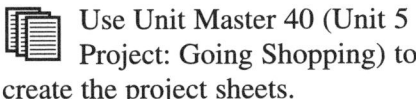

Learners apply the vocabulary and concepts from the unit to collect information about prices in local supermarkets.

Get Ready

Use Unit Master 40 (Unit 5 Project: Going Shopping) to create the project sheets.
- In the blank column headings write three common food items (e.g., apples, chicken, milk).
- Copy the master and distribute to learners.

Do the Work

- Ask each learner to fill in the name and address of the supermarket he or she will use for the project.
- Have learners visit a supermarket or read its ads and take notes on the prices for the items listed on their project sheets. They can write the prices on their project sheets at home or in class.

Present Your Project

- Write the three project food items on the board or an overhead transparency.
- Have learners ask each other where they shopped and what the prices were for the three items.
- Write this information on the board or the transparency.
- Encourage discussion of the supermarkets. Ask learners which is the best place to shop and why.

Technology Extra

- Ask learners to bring calculators from home, or use class sets if you have them.
- Review the keys and functions on the calculator introduced in the Unit 4 Technology Extra.
- Have learners calculate the total cost of the food items listed on their project sheets.

One Step Up
Have learners check their calculator work by adding the figures on a piece of paper.

 Assign Workbook p. 49 (Check Your Progress).

 Use Unit Master 41 (Unit 5 Checkup/Review) whenever you complete this unit.

Unit 6: Hurry Up!

Materials for the Unit

- Articles of clothing listed in lesson vocabulary
- Clothing and accessory ads from catalogs or newspapers
- Pictures showing different kinds of weather
- Pictures of the sites in the Picture Dictionary on p. 79
- Disposable cameras
- Card stock in two colors
- Vocabulary Card Masters for Unit 6
- Local maps
- Small sticky notes
- Unit Masters 42–47
- Customizable Masters 1 and 3
- Generic Assessment Masters 7 and 8

Hurry Up!

Follow these steps to discuss the unit title:

- Walk slowly around the room.
- Say *hurry up* and walk more quickly.
- Do this several times, moving more quickly after each prompt.
- Ask two learners to walk around the room. Say *hurry up* while they are walking.
- If the command does not elicit the right response, demonstrate again and repeat until learners move quickly at the command.

Photo

Follow the suggestions on p. 5 for talking about the photo. Read the question below the arrow aloud and ask these *either/or* questions:

- Is this a woman or a man?
- Is this a minivan or a bus?
- Is the door open or closed?
- Is this a girl or a boy?
- Is this a girl or a boy?
- Are they adults or children?
- Is it rainy or sunny?
- Do the children have hats or umbrellas?

Caption

- Read the caption below the photo aloud several times and have learners repeat it after you.
- Draw a picture of a rainy day if necessary.
- Ask learners, "Is today rainy?"

<u>Class Story</u>

See the suggestions on p. 8 about writing class stories using a photo.

72 Unit 6

Picture Dictionary

Follow the suggestions on p. 6 for introducing vocabulary.

Follow the suggestions on p. 6 for using vocabulary cards. Use the Vocabulary Card Masters for the words in the Picture Dictionary and card stock or paper to prepare pictures of the weather conditions listed. Then prepare corresponding word cards.

Do a class matching activity. Tape the pictures to the board and have learners tape the correct words under the pictures.

Activity A

Follow the suggestions on p. 6 for writing activities.

<u>Answers</u>
1. rainy   5. windy
2. cold   6. cloudy
3. sunny   7. cool
4. hot   8. snowy

In the US

Point to pictures that represent a variety of nice weather conditions and have learners say, "Nice day." To establish the meaning of "It sure is!" do the following:
- Write *It sure is!* on the board. Write an equal sign and the word *yes*. Point to each side of the equation and nod your head *yes*.
- Show learners pictures of weather conditions again and say *nice day*. Learners should nod *yes* or *no* according to the photo.
- Show the pictures and say *nice day* again. This time, have learners say *It sure is!* if the picture shows nice weather.

<u>One Step Up</u>
Say or spell the weather vocabulary words while learners write them.

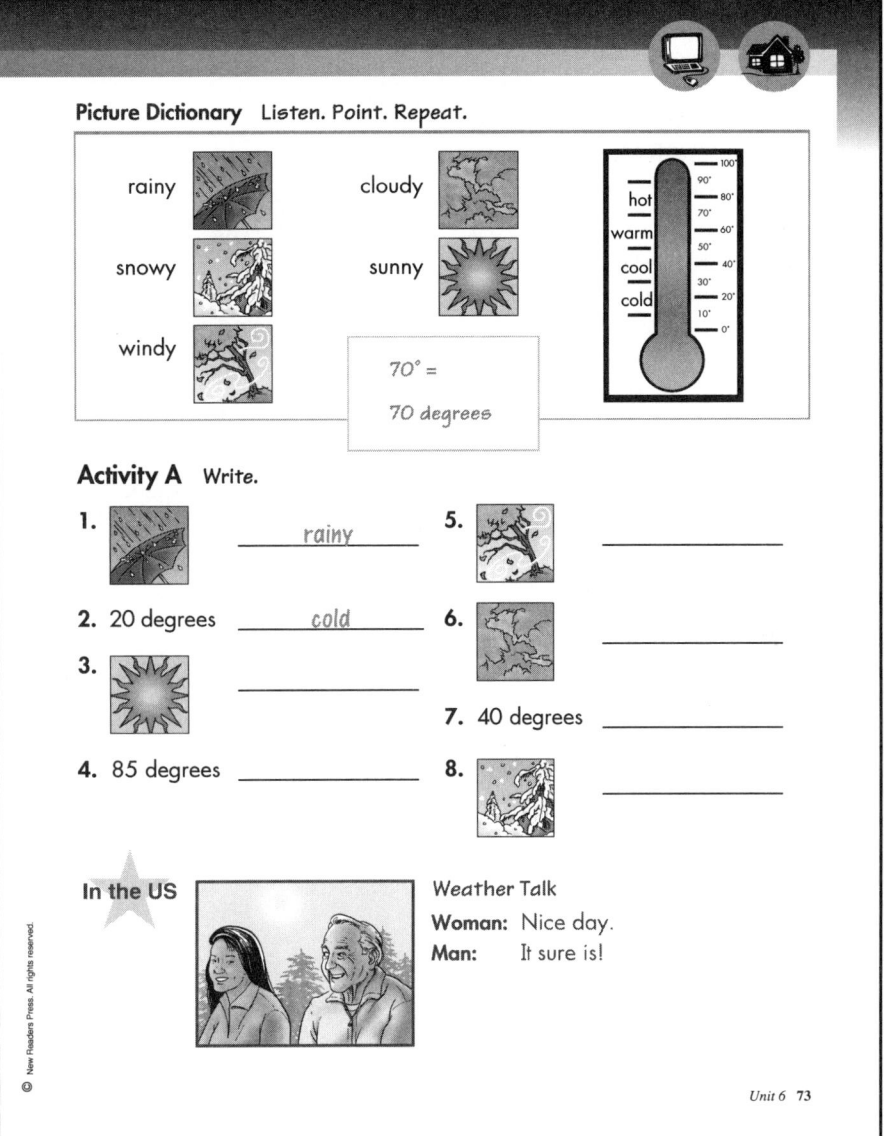

<u>Extension</u>
For homework, have learners watch the news on television. It may help if you tell them which television stations to watch and at what times.
- Ask learners to write the weather and temperature for the next day.
- Have them report back to the class the next time you meet.

Unit 6 73

Lesson 1: I'm Wet!

I'm Wet!
Have learners read the lesson number and title. To establish the meaning of *wet*, put some water in a cup, sprinkle some on your arm or hand, and say, "I'm wet."

Photo
Read the caption and have learners repeat it several times. Follow the suggestions on p. 5 for talking about the photo. Then ask the following questions:
- Who is this?
- What is she doing?
- Where is she going?
- Does she have an umbrella?
- What's the weather like? *or* How's the weather?
- Is she wearing a coat?
- Is she wet?

<u>Class Story</u>
Using the answers to the above questions, write a class story. Write the sentences below on the board, leaving a blank for each word the learners selected.

Your story may look like this:
*The weather is <u>rainy.</u>
Mrs. Gupta is walking to the <u>Westside Medical Clinic.</u>
She doesn't have an <u>umbrella.</u>
She's <u>wet.</u>
She's not <u>happy.</u>*

Follow the suggestions on p. 8 (Steps 3–7) for using Class Stories.

Comprehension
Follow the suggestions on p. 6 for listening/reading comprehension.

 Play the audio or read the listening script below and have learners circle the words they hear. Circulate to monitor learners' work.

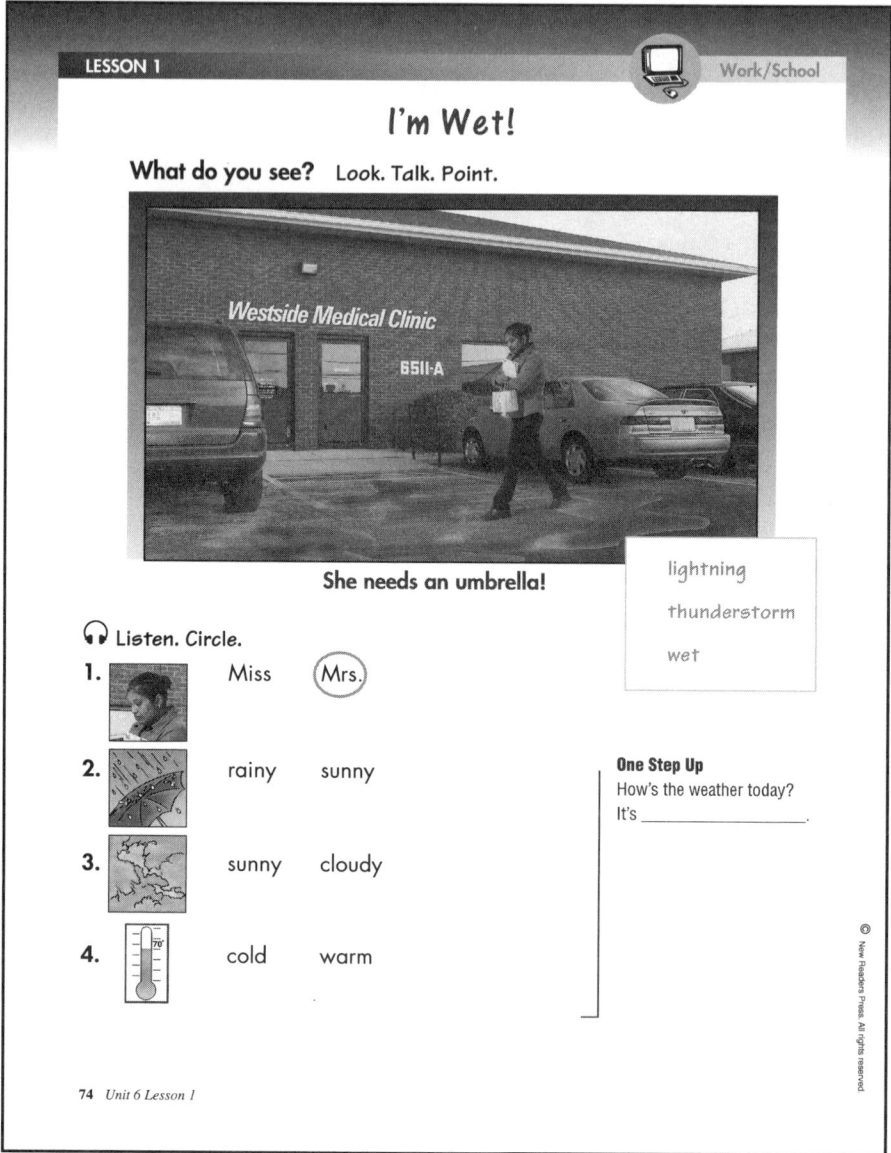

<u>Listening Script</u>
Listen. Circle.
1. This is Mrs. Gupta.
2. It's rainy.
3. It's cloudy.
4. It's warm.

<u>Answers</u>
1. Mrs. 3. cloudy
2. rainy 4. warm

Assign Workbook p. 50.

Picture Dictionary

Follow the suggestions on p. 6 for introducing vocabulary.

Follow the suggestions on p. 6 for using vocabulary cards. Use the Vocabulary Card Masters for the words in the Picture Dictionary.
- Bring in examples of the articles of clothing listed.
- Pass out cards or sticky notes with the vocabulary words and have learners affix them to the correct articles of clothing.

Activity A

Play the audio or read the listening script below. Follow the suggestions on p. 6 for listening activities.

Listening Script/Answers
Listen. Circle.
1. skirt   4. raincoat
2. sweater   5. coat
3. boots   6. jacket

One Step Up

After learners write the words for the clothes they are wearing, write the words on the board. Have learners tell you how to put them in alphabetical order.

Class Chat

Use Customizable Master 3 (3-Column Chart). Follow the suggestions on p. 7 (Preparing for a Class Chat) for customizing and duplicating the master and distributing the copies.

Follow the suggestions on p. 7 for facilitating a Class Chat.

Extension
Teach or review *does/doesn't*. Follow the suggestions on p. 7 for Class Chat Follow-Ups. Then do the following:
- Have learners read the follow-up sentences they wrote to a partner, their group, or the class.

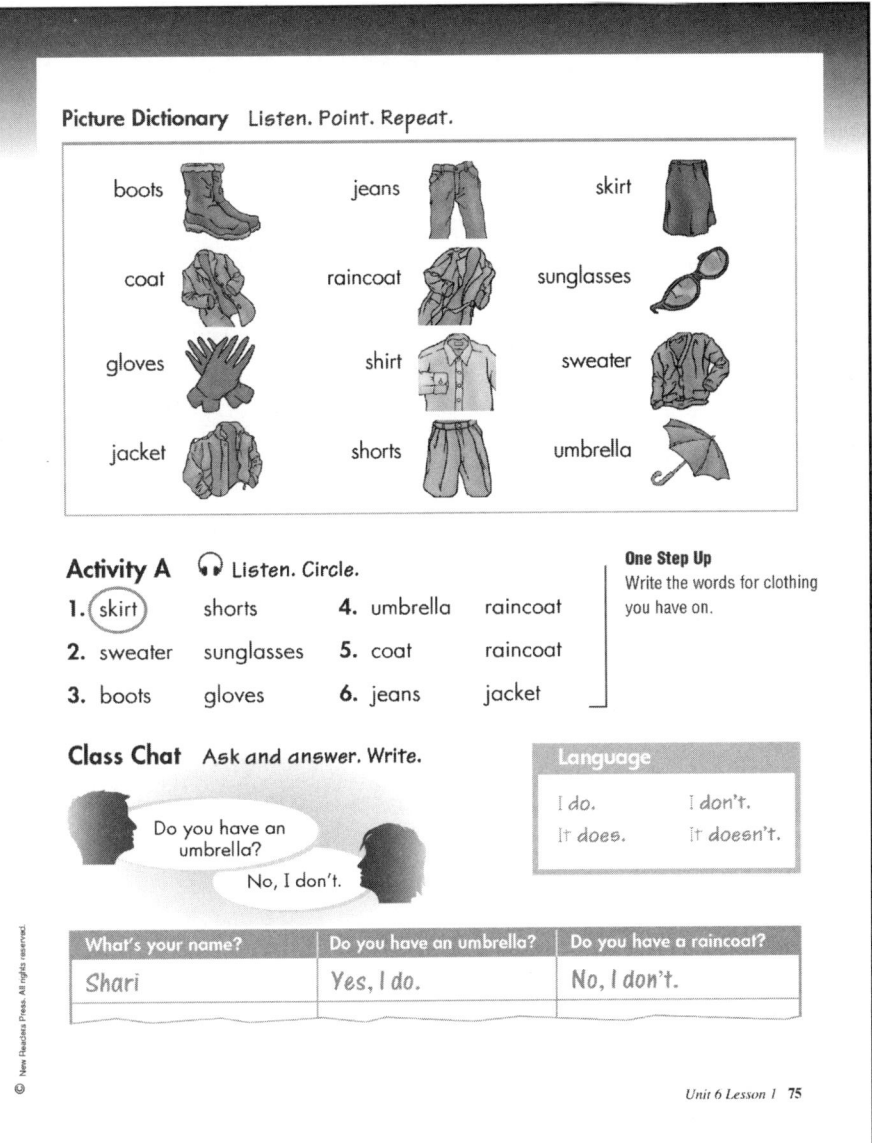

- Use the sentences to write a class story on the board or an overhead transparency.
- Have learners read the story aloud several times.
- Ask questions such as, "Does Juan have a raincoat?" Learners respond *yes* or *no* according to the sentences on the board.

One Step Up
Following the model in the Class Chat, have learners use the vocabulary from this page to form questions about articles of clothing. Then have learners ask a partner the questions.

Extension
To combine reading ads with the vocabulary in this lesson, bring in ads for clothing items and accessories cut from catalogs or newspaper ads. Have learners ask and answer questions based on the ads (e.g., How much are sunglasses? $9.89).

Use Customizable Master 1 (Bingo Chart) to review the vocabulary from the first four pages of this unit.

Activity B

🎧 Review the suggestions on p. 6 for listening to the audio program, then play the audio or read the listening script below. Pause at the end of each sentence to allow time for learners to circle the weather and clothing words they hear.

<u>Listening Script/Answers</u>
Listen. Circle.
1. It's sunny. Wear sunglasses today. *(sunny, sunglasses)*
2. It's cold. Wear your gloves. *(cold, gloves)*
3. It's rainy. Take an umbrella. *(rainy, umbrella)*
4. It's hot. Wear shorts. *(hot, shorts)*
5. It's rainy. Take a raincoat. *(rainy, raincoat)*

<u>Extension</u>
Play this listening game to review two-digit numbers. Be sure to model the game before playing so learners understand what to do.
- Say a two-digit number (e.g., 17).
- The next person says a two-digit number that begins with the second digit of the first number (e.g., 75).
- The next person says a two-digit number that begins with the second digit of that number (e.g., 54.) The game continues, with each player saying a two-digit number that begins with the last digit of the previous number.
- When a learner is not listening or says an incorrect number, that person is "out."
- The winner is the last person in the game.

Activity C

Follow the suggestions on p. 8 for pair dictations.
- Have partner A begin the activity by reading the first set of temperatures while partner B writes.
- Then have partner B read the second set of temperatures while partner A writes.

Activity B 🎧 Listen. Circle.

	Weather		Clothing	
1.	(sunny)	windy	boots	(sunglasses)
2.	cold	warm	gloves	shorts
3.	cold	rainy	umbrella	jacket
4.	hot	rainy	jeans	shorts
5.	rainy	sunny	raincoat	shorts

Activity C Listen to a partner. Don't look. Write.

Partner A Speaks	Partner B Writes	Partner B Speaks	Partner A Writes
1. 45°	45°	1. 25°	
2. 87°		2. 33°	
3. 55°		3. 78°	
4. 91°		4. 51°	
5. 62°		5. 49°	

TASK 1 The Weather

Watch or listen to the news. Write or draw pictures of the weather for this week.

One Step Up
Write or draw pictures of your clothing for this week.

Sun.	Mon.	Tues.	Wed.	Thurs.	Fri.	Sat.

76 *Unit 6 Lesson 1*

Task 1

Have learners practice writing or drawing pictures about the weather in class before doing the task at home.
- Make a class chart like the one in the student book, showing seven columns and two rows.
- Label the first row with the days of the week.
- Write or draw the weather for each day in the second row.
- Check learners' charts at the beginning of each class and enter the appropriate weather words into the class chart.

After the chart is completed, talk about the weather. Ask questions such as, "How was the weather on Tuesday?"

One Step Up

Have learners draw pictures or write the names of the clothes they wore this week. With a partner, in a small group, or as a large group, ask and answer questions such as, "What did you wear on Thursday?"

 Assign Workbook pp. 51–52.

<u>Extension</u>
Follow the suggestions for playing Concentration on p. 9.

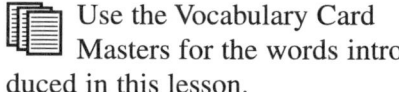 Use the Vocabulary Card Masters for the words introduced in this lesson.

Have learners play in groups of four.

Lesson 2: I Need the Car

Photos

Read the lesson title and have learners repeat it several times.

Follow the suggestions on p. 5 for talking about photos.

Point to the speech bubble in each photo frame and have learners repeat the words aloud. Then ask learners these questions:

Photo 1
- Is Mrs. Gupta in the kitchen or the living room?
- Is she talking to her children or her husband?
- Is it morning or night?
- Does Mr. Gupta want the van today or tomorrow?

Photo 2
- Is Mrs. Gupta reading a book or talking on a phone?
- Is she talking to a man or a woman?
- Is the woman her friend or her husband?
- Does the woman say, "Walk with me tomorrow" or "Ride with me tomorrow"?

Photo 3
- Are they adults or children?
- Are they going to school or to work?
- Are they getting into a car or a bus?
- Is the bus yellow or blue?
- Do they like to ride the bus?

Photo 4
- Is this Mr. Gupta or Mrs. Gupta?
- Is he in a van or a bus?
- Is he going fast or slow?
- Is he happy or angry?

Attention Box

Ride is generally used when a person is a *passenger* in a vehicle, e.g., *ride the bus*. One common exception to this rule is *take the train*. This differentiation may be difficult to convey to learners, so you may want to have them simply memorize the expressions.

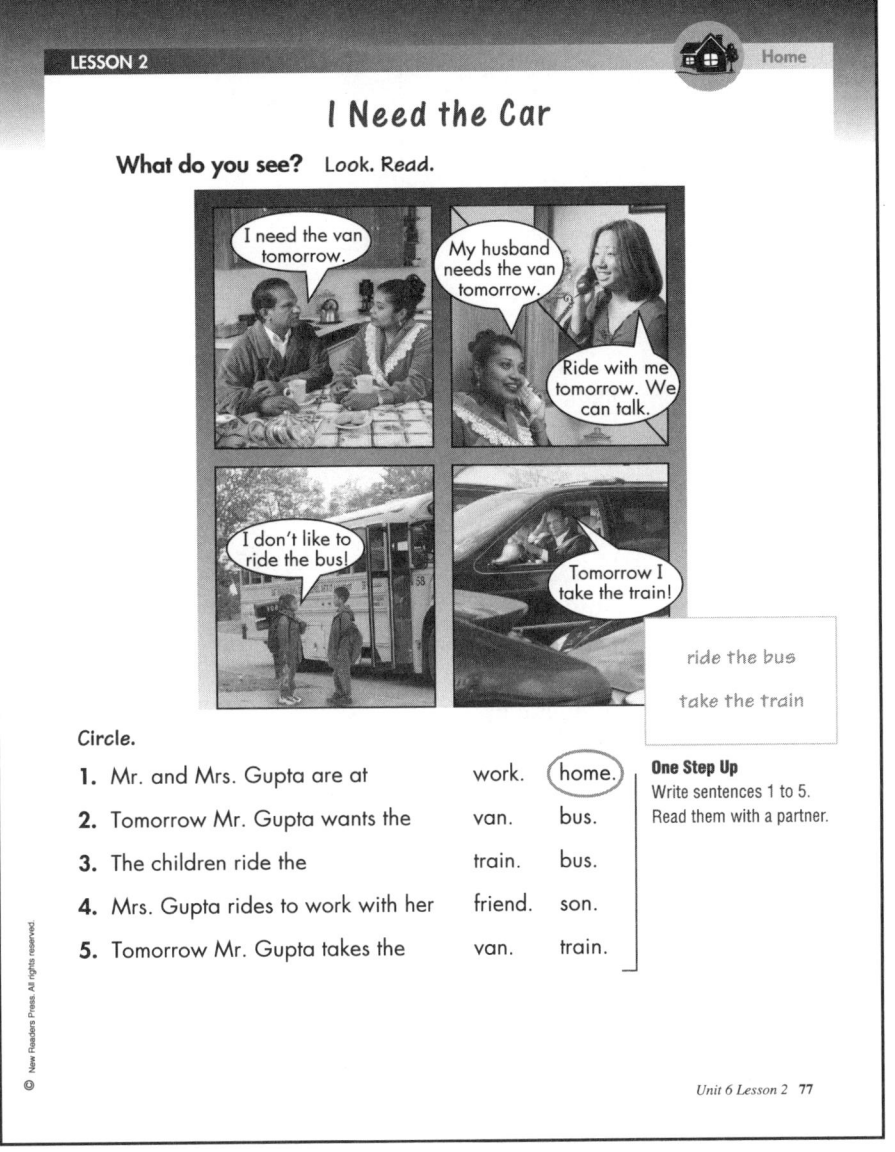

Comprehension

Follow the suggestions on p. 6 for listening/reading comprehension. Before beginning this activity, read the first sentence aloud for the class, emphasizing *home*. Then do the following:
- Demonstrate on the board or an overhead transparency that the word should be circled.
- Read the second sentence aloud and have learners say the correct answer.
- Have them circle it in their books and complete the exercise.
- If learners seem confused, do the activity together as a group.
- Circulate while learners circle the words that complete each sentence.
- Have learners read the completed sentences together several times.

Answers
1. home   3. bus   5. train
2. van   4. friend

One Step Up

Monitor learners while they write the sentences. Check for capital letters and punctuation.

Assign Workbook p. 53, Exercise A.

Unit 6 *Lesson 2* 77

Picture Dictionary

Follow the suggestions on p. 6 for introducing vocabulary.

Follow the suggestions on p. 6 for using vocabulary cards. Use the Vocabulary Card Masters for the words in the Picture Dictionary.

Language

Before beginning, explain the phrase *get a ride*. Tell learners not to say, "Ride a car." Then follow these steps:

- Reproduce the chart on the board.
- Have learners repeat all the combinations several times.
- Ask questions such as, "Do people drive trains?" (Do not use the personal pronoun *you* in these questions because learners may think you are asking what they do personally.)

Class Chat

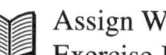 Use Customizable Master 3 (3-Column Chart). Follow the suggestions on p. 7 (Preparing for a Class Chat) for customizing and duplicating the master and distributing the copies.

Follow the suggestions on p. 7 for facilitating Class Chats.

Explain that even if learners do not drive a car themselves but get a ride, they can answer *yes* for *drive to school*.

Learners should be ready now to be introduced to questions beginning with *do* or *does*. This usage can be very difficult for learners who come from languages that do not use auxiliaries for questions. Learners should not be expected to master *do* and *does* at this point; this is just the beginning of their practice.

This language activity also reviews personal pronouns and provides practice in chart-reading comprehension.

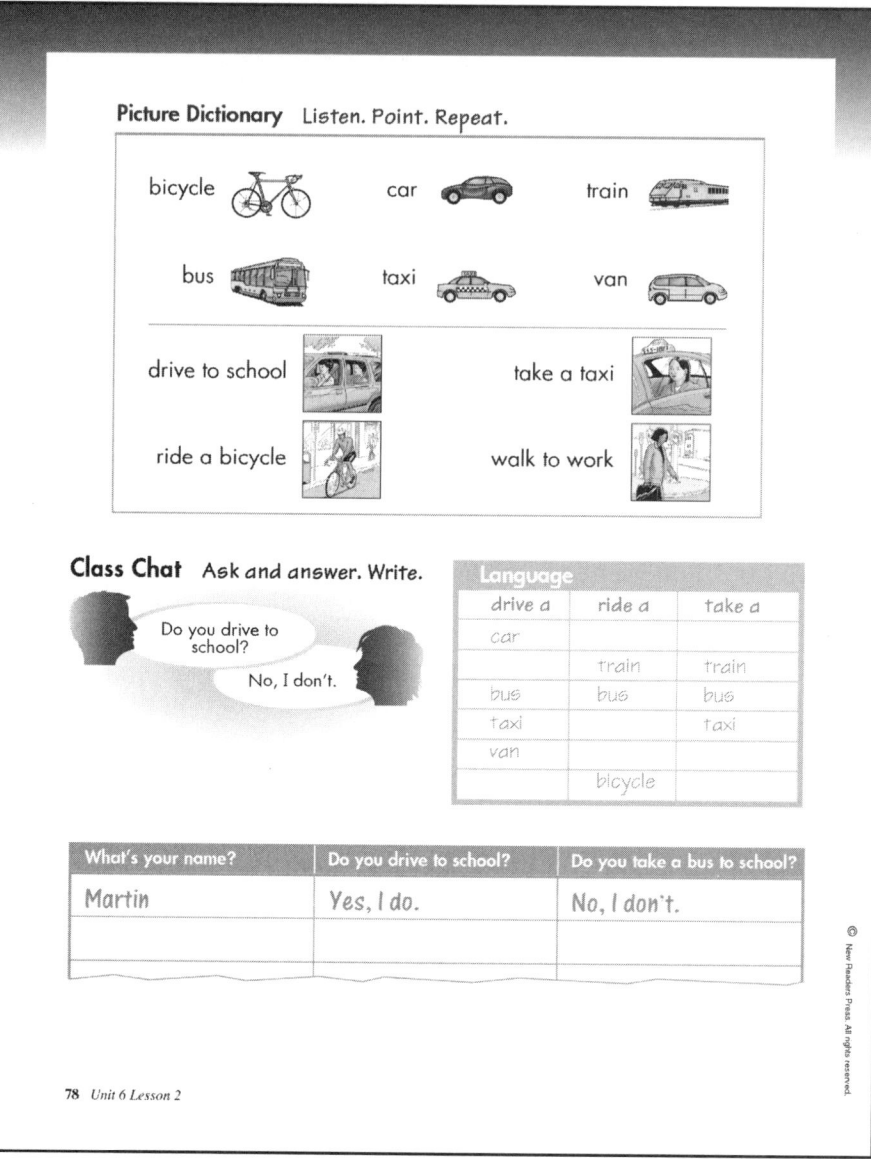

Extension

Follow the suggestions on p. 7 for Class Chat Follow-Ups.

- After learners write sentences about the chat, have them read their sentences to a partner or a group.
- Use the sentences to write a class story.
- Type the story, duplicate it, and give it to learners to read the next time your class meets. This will serve as a review.

Assign Workbook p. 53, Exercise B, and p. 54.

Use the Vocabulary Card Masters for the words introduced on this page to play Concentration. Follow the suggestions on p. 9 for playing this game.

78 Unit 6 *Lesson 2*

Picture Dictionary

Before beginning this activity, you may want to take some pictures of sites mentioned in the Picture Dictionary. It will be especially helpful if these sites are located in the neighborhood where you teach.

Follow the suggestions on p. 6 for introducing vocabulary.

Follow the suggestions on p. 6 for using vocabulary cards. Use the Vocabulary Card Masters for the words in the Picture Dictionary.

Activity A

Follow the suggestions on p. 7 for writing activities.

Answers
1. bus stop
2. police department
3. clinic
4. train station
5. railroad crossing
6. stop
7. construction

Extensions
1. Take the class on a short field trip. Walk around the neighborhood where you teach and ask learners to identify the places and signs that they see.
2. Divide learners into groups of three to five. Give each group a disposable camera and have them take pictures of places and signs in the community. Develop the film, return the photos to the groups, and have them talk or write about the photos.

One Step Up
Suggest that learners look for signs on the way to work or school and draw two of them.
- Post the hand-drawn signs on the walls of the classroom.
- Give learners time to walk around and look at each other's work.
- Have learners ask and answer questions about the signs with a partner.

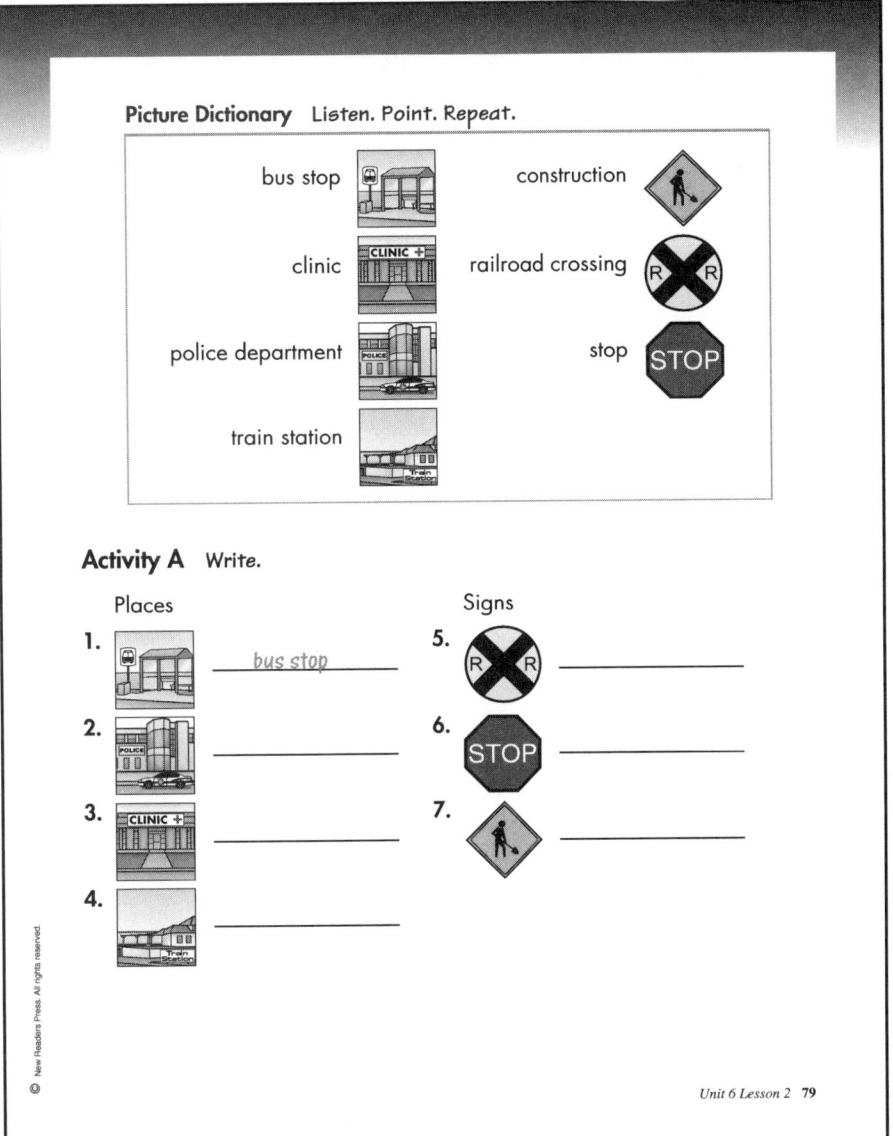

Assign Workbook p. 55.

Use Unit Masters 42 (Reading: The Letter *S*), 43 (Reading: The Letter *R*), 44 (Life Skills: Organize Information), and 45 (Game: Match the Words) now or at any time during the rest of the unit.

Master 45
Copy the master on card stock and give one set of cards to each group. Change the level of difficulty for this game by varying the color of the card stock used for duplicating the master.

- To make the game less difficult, use two different colors of card stock, one for the cards in Column 1 and another for the cards in Column 2.
- To make the game more challenging, copy all the cards onto the same color.

Unit 6 *Lesson 2* 79

Activity B

Follow the suggestions on p. 5 for talking about photos. Before reading the story, ask these questions:
- Who is it?
- What is she doing?
- How's the weather?
- What does the sign say?
- Does Mrs. Gupta stop?
- Does the car stop?
- How does Mrs. Gupta feel?

Read the story aloud several times while learners listen. Then do the following:
- Read the story with the group several times.
- Do a round-robin in which each learner reads a line of the story.
- Repeat the story until every learner has read a line.

Activity C

Follow the suggestions on p. 7 for writing activities.
- Before learners do the writing activity, have them answer the questions aloud using short answers.
- Have learners write the short answers in their books.
- Model the activity using long answers in the form of complete sentences. Have learners give long answers aloud.

Answers
1. Rainy and cool.
2. No.
3. Yes.
4. Yes.
5. No.

One Step Up

You may want to have more advanced learners write the long answers in addition to or as an alternative to the short ones.

Task 2

Before assigning the task, show learners a variety of maps. Then follow these steps:
- Draw a map of the classroom on the board. Start with a large outline, establish orientation, and have learners draw items on the map.
- There may be evacuation or fire drill maps in your room. Point these out.
- Tell learners that if they work, they should read their workplace maps too. This is important in case of emergencies.

Model Task 2 to make sure learners understand what to do.
- Post learners' completed maps on the board or wall of the classroom.
- Have them circulate and admire each other's efforts.

One Step Up

Have learners complete the sentences. Remind them that if they get a ride anyplace, they can use, "I drive."

Have learners read their sentences to a partner, a group, or the class.

Extension

If computers are available, have learners type the sentences.

Activity B Read.

Mrs. Gupta's Day
It's rainy. It's cool.
Mrs. Gupta walks to the clinic.
She doesn't have an umbrella.
Mrs. Gupta has a raincoat.
She is at a stop sign. A car doesn't stop.

Activity C Write.
1. What's the weather? ____Rainy____ and ____cool____.
2. Does Mrs. Gupta have an umbrella? _____.
3. Does Mrs. Gupta have a raincoat? _____.
4. Does she walk to the clinic? _____.
5. Does the car stop? _____.

TASK 2 A Map of Your Community
Draw a map of your community. Write the names of places and signs on the map.

One Step Up
Write ways you get to places in your community.
1. I walk to _____.
2. I drive to _____.
3. I take a _____ to the _____.
4. I ride a _____ to the _____.

Remember?
drive, get a ride, walk, bicycle, bus, taxi

Unit 6 Project

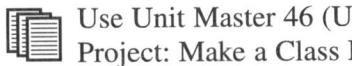 Use Generic Assessment Masters 7 (Oral Communication Rubric) and 8 (Written Communication Rubric) to evaluate learner performance on the Unit 6 Project.

Learners use a local map to prepare a map showing their own community. If they do not all live in the same community, divide them into groups based on proximity to where they live.

Have available a supply of small sticky notes.

Get Ready

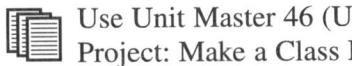 Use Unit Master 46 (Unit 6 Project: Make a Class Map).

- Divide learners into groups of four or five.
- Assign roles of recorder, reporter, timekeeper, and materials gatherer in each group.
- Duplicate one copy of the master for each group and distribute to the materials gatherers.

Do the Work

- Have the timekeepers record starting and ending times for each stage of their group's project.
- Have learners in each group work together to find their addresses on a local map.
- Have the group recorders print the name and address of each group member on a sticky note.
- Monitor the groups to ensure that they are working together to complete the task.

Present Your Project

- Each group reporter presents the address for each learner in his or her group.
- The reporter puts the sticky note in the right place on the group map.

This activity can facilitate ride sharing or carpooling. It may also encourage learners who live close to one another to form study or practice groups.

Technology Extra

Ask for permission before learners type a class list. Some learners may not want to share their addresses and phone numbers.

Extension

Have learners type their names, addresses, and phone numbers, then duplicate them on labels or business cards. Again, because of privacy concerns, not everyone may want to participate in this extension.

 Assign Workbook p. 56 (Check Your Progress).

Use Unit Master 47 (Unit 6 Checkup/Review) whenever you complete this unit.

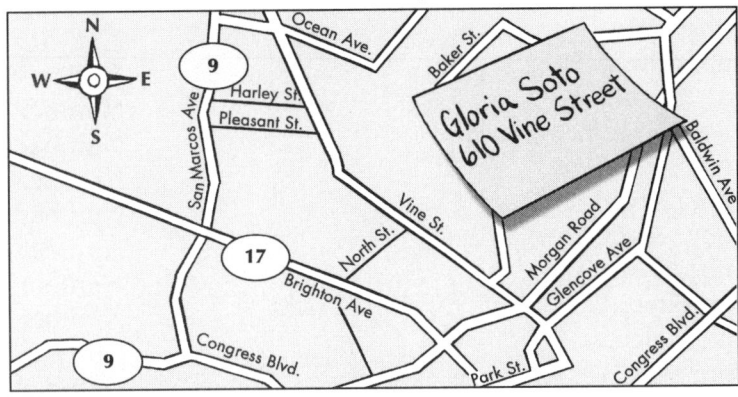

UNIT 6 Project

A Class Map

Get Ready
Get in groups of four or five. Get a small map of your community from your teacher. Find the addresses of students on the map.

Do the Work
Write class names and addresses on sticky notes.

Present Your Project
Make group reports. The group reporter says: "_____ lives here." The reporter puts the sticky note on the map. The reporter does this for every student in the group.

Technology Extra
Use the computer to type a class list of names and addresses. Save the list. If students give you their phone numbers, add them to your list.

Unit 6 Project 81

Listening Scripts

This section contains scripts for the content of the audiotape and audio CD for *English—No Problem!* literacy level.

Warm-Up Unit A
Cecile's Day

Lesson 1, Page 11

Activity B
Listen. Circle. Write.
Number one. C
Number two. F
Number three. B
Number four. D
Number five. E
Number six. G
Number seven. C
Number eight. F
Number nine. A
Number ten. E
Number eleven. G
Number twelve. A

Lesson 2, Page 12

Activity B
Listen. Circle. Write.
Number one. J
Number two. K
Number three. N
Number four. I
Number five. P
Number six. H
Number seven. J
Number eight. L
Number nine. I
Number ten. M
Number eleven. O
Number twelve. N

Lesson 3, Page 13

Activity B
Listen. Circle. Write.
Number one. S
Number two. V
Number three. U
Number four. Q
Number five. Q
Number six. U
Number seven. T

Number eight. R
Number nine. U
Number ten. S
Number eleven. S
Number twelve. V

Lesson 4, Page 14

Activity B
Listen. Circle. Write.
Number one. Y
Number two. W
Number three. Z
Number four. X
Number five. Z
Number six. X
Number seven. Z
Number eight. Y
Number nine. W

Lesson 5, Page 15

Activity A
Listen. Write.
Zero
One
Two
Three
Four
Five
Six
Seven
Eight
Nine
Ten

Lesson 5, Page 15

Activity B
Listen. Circle. Write.
Number one. 2
Number two. 6
Number three. 8
Number four. 1
Number five. 3
Number six. 7
Number seven. 5
Number eight. 10

82 Listening Scripts

Number nine. 4
Number ten. 0 [zero]
Number eleven. 9
Number twelve. 4

Warm-Up Unit B
Omar's Day

Lesson 1, Page 17

Activity B
Listen. Circle. Write.
Number one. b
Number two. f
Number three. e
Number four. g
Number five. d
Number six. a
Number seven. c
Number eight. f
Number nine. g
Number ten. c
Number eleven. b
Number twelve. a

Lesson 2, Page 18

Activity B
Listen. Circle. Write.
Number one. h
Number two. k
Number three. o
Number four. p
Number five. n
Number six. l
Number seven. j
Number eight. k
Number nine. i
Number ten. m
Number eleven. o
Number twelve. i

Lesson 3, Page 19

Activity B
Listen. Circle. Write.
Number one. t
Number two. v
Number three. r
Number four. q
Number five. q
Number six. u
Number seven. t
Number eight. r
Number nine. u
Number ten. v
Number eleven. s
Number twelve. v

Lesson 4, Page 20

Activity B
Listen. Circle. Write.
Number one. y
Number two. z
Number three. w
Number four. z
Number five. w
Number six. x
Number seven. x
Number eight. y
Number nine. z

Unit 1
Welcome!

Lesson 1, Page 24

Marina at School
What do you see? Look. Listen. Point.
Number one. Marina is in school. She's in the school office. Marina reads the classroom number.
Number two. Marina is in the classroom. The teacher speaks to Marina. "Welcome to English class!"

Lesson 1, Page 25

Activity A
Listen. Circle.
Number one. Circle check. Check.
Number two. Circle listen. Listen.
Number three. Circle write. Write.
Number four. Circle pencil. Pencil.
Number five. Circle book. Book.
Number six. Circle speak. Speak.

Listening Scripts 83

Lesson 1, Page 25

Activity B
Listen. Check.
Number one. Teacher. Check teacher.
Number two. Pen. Check pen.
Number three. Circle. Check circle.
Number four. Student. Check student.

Unit 2
Smile!

Lesson 1, Page 34

What do you see? Look. Listen. Point.
Number one. I'm a husband. I'm a father.
Number two. I'm a husband. I'm a grandfather.
Number three. I'm a daughter. I'm a sister.
Number four. I'm a wife. I'm a mother.
Number five. I'm a wife. I'm a grandmother.
Number six. I'm a son. I'm a brother.

Lesson 1, Page 35

Activity A
Listen. Circle.
Number one. grandmother
Number two. granddaughter
Number three. grandchild
Number four. Mr. Lewis

Lesson 1, Page 36

Activity B
Listen. Write numbers.
Letter a. 27
Letter b. 23
Letter c. 21
Letter d. 28
Letter e. 26
Letter f. 24
Letter g. 30
Letter h. 22
Letter i. 29
Letter j. 25

Lesson 2, Page 39

In the US
Show ID at work.
Listen. Repeat. Practice.
Guard: Your ID, please.
Ben: Excuse me?
Guard: Your ID, please.
Ben: Here.
Guard: OK. Thank you.
Ben: You're welcome.

Unit 3
You're Sick

Lesson 1, Page 44

Your Daughter Is Sick
What do you see? Look. Listen. Point.
Nurse: Your daughter is sick.
Dyna: What's wrong?
Nurse: She has a fever.
Dyna: Excuse me? Please repeat.
Nurse: A fever.
Dyna: Oh, I see.

Lesson 1, Page 45

Activity A
Listen. Write.
Number one. head, head
Number two. nose, nose
Number three. mouth, mouth
Number four. arm, arm
Number five. foot, foot
Number six. eye, eye
Number seven. ear, ear
Number eight. stomach, stomach
Number nine. hand, hand
Number ten. leg, leg

Lesson 1, Page 46

Activity B
Listen. Circle.
What's wrong?

Number one.
My head hurts.
What hurts?
My head.

Number two.
O-oh [*moan*], my leg.
What's wrong?
My leg hurts.

Number three.
I have a stomachache.
Where does it hurt?
Here in my stomach.

Number four.
Ouch! My hand.
What hurts?
My hand!

Number five.
Mommy . . . my eye hurts.
What's wrong, honey?
My eye hurts.

Unit 4
Money, Money, Money!

Page 53

Activity A
Listen. Circle.
Number one. coin
Number two. change
Number three. money order
Number four. amount
Number five. sign
Number six. cash

Lesson 1, Page 55

Activity A
Listen. Circle.
Number one. dime
Number two. penny
Number three. fifty
Number four. ten
Number five. five
Number six. one dollar

Lesson 1, Page 56

Activity B
Listen. Write numbers.
Letter a. 85
Letter b. 70
Letter c. 61
Letter d. 90
Letter e. 97
Letter f. 60
Letter g. 72
Letter h. 80

Lesson 1, Page 56

Activity C
Listen. Write words.
Letter a. sixty-one
Letter b. seventy-two
Letter c. ninety
Letter d. seventy
Letter e. eighty-five
Letter f. eighty
Letter g. sixty
Letter h. ninety-seven

Lesson 2, Page 57

Armando's First Paycheck
What do you see? Look. Listen. Point. Repeat.
Number one. CBA Company—company name
Number two. 8/6/04—date
Number three. $360.09 [*three hundred sixty dollars and nine cents*] —amount in numbers
Number four. Three hundred sixty dollars and nine cents—amount in words
Number five. Armando Diaz—pay to
Number six. James A. Curran—signature

Lesson 2, Page 59

In the US
Show ID to cash a check.
Listen. Repeat. Practice.
Cashier: May I see your picture ID?
Armando: Excuse me?
Cashier: May I see your picture ID?
Armando: OK.
Cashier: Thanks.

Unit 5
No Milk

Lesson 1, Page 64

Grocery Shopping
What do you see? Look. Listen. Point.
Greg and his wife, Ann, are at the supermarket. Their children are with them. They are in the dairy section. The wife is buying milk. There are eggs, butter, and milk in this part of the supermarket.

Lesson 1, Page 64

Listen. Circle.
Number one. Milk. Circle milk. Milk.
Number two. Daughter. Circle daughter. Daughter.
Number three. Eggs. Circle eggs. Eggs.
Number four. Butter. Circle butter. Butter.

Lesson 1, Page 65

Activity A
Listen. Circle.
Number one. tomatoes, tomatoes
Number two. apples, apples
Number three. potatoes, potatoes
Number four. oranges, oranges
Number five. shrimp, shrimp
Number six. carrots, carrots
Number seven. beef, beef
Number eight. fish, fish
Now copy the words.

Lesson 1, Page 66

Activity B
Listen. Write.
Letter a.   Do you need coffee?
Coffee? Yes!
Letter b.   Do you like noodles?
Noodles? Yes!
Letter c.   Do you want tea?
Tea? Yes, please.
Letter d.   Do you need water?
I'd love water!
Letter e.   Do you need oil?
Oil? Yes, please.
Letter f.   Do you like beans?
Beans? No!
Letter g.   Do you want more rice?
Rice? Yes, please.
Letter h.   Do you like bread?
Bread? Yes.
Letter i.   Do you need juice?
Juice? Yes, I do.

Unit 6
Hurry Up!

Lesson 1, Page 74

Listen. Circle.
Number one. This is Mrs. Gupta *[Goop-tuh—first syllable is like the* u *in truth]*.
Number two. It's rainy.
Number three. It's cloudy.
Number four. It's warm.

Lesson 1, Page 75

Activity A
Listen. Circle
Number one. skirt
Number two. sweater
Number three. boots
Number four. raincoat
Number five. coat
Number six. jacket

Lesson 1, Page 76

Activity B
Listen. Circle.
Number one. It's sunny. Wear sunglasses today.
Number two. It's cold. Wear your gloves.
Number three. It's rainy. Take an umbrella.
Number four. It's hot. Wear shorts.
Number five. It's rainy. Take a raincoat.

Working with Maps

When working with literacy level learners, take into consideration that maps are highly symbolic objects. At this level, some learners may have had little or no experience using maps, so the concept of a map will need to be introduced before working with the maps in this appendix. Nonetheless, map literacy is an important skill and should be included in your instruction.

One way to introduce maps is to use a map that would be familiar to everyone in the classroom—a map of the classroom itself. Draw this map on the board or an overhead transparency, showing where the door is, the chairs, the desks, and anything else that helps illustrate the room. Then draw a map of the building where the classroom is located, showing how a map can help someone find his or her way around the building. These maps should be created in front of the learners and with their help. If you are also able to draw a map of your neighborhood and town or city, you will further reinforce this skill.

Once your learners understand the concept of a map, you can begin using the maps in this appendix. Try using a map when learners initiate topics about their home countries or about items in the news.

This page provides suggestions specific to the map of the United States as well as to the map of the world.

US Map

Use this US map to show learners where their state and city are located. Ask them what state they live in, what other states they know about, and in what states they have friends or relatives.

- When appropriate, use the map to show where the characters in the student book live or where learners think they live.
- Addresses are referred to throughout the student book and workbook in stories (particularly in Unit 2), school registration forms, medical forms, and elsewhere. Refer learners to the US map at each of these points. Ask them to find the city and/or state on the map.
- When talking about the weather (Unit 6) refer learners to the US map. Ask: Is it rainy in California today? How is the weather today in California? How is the weather today in New York? Is it warm or cold?

World Map

Use the world map as a way to welcome new learners into your class.

- Post a large world map on a bulletin board in your room. Have learners come up to the board and point to where they came from and where they are now.
- Take a Polaroid picture of each learner. Learners can write their names at the bottom of their pictures. Using a piece of yarn, pin one end of the yarn to the town they live in now and pin the other end to the town they came from, along with the picture of the learner. As new learners join your class, add their pictures to the map in the same way.
- When talking about the weather (in Unit 6) refer learners to the world map. Ask: Is it rainy in your home country today? How is the weather today in Mexico? How is the weather today in Ukraine? Is it warm or cold?

US Map

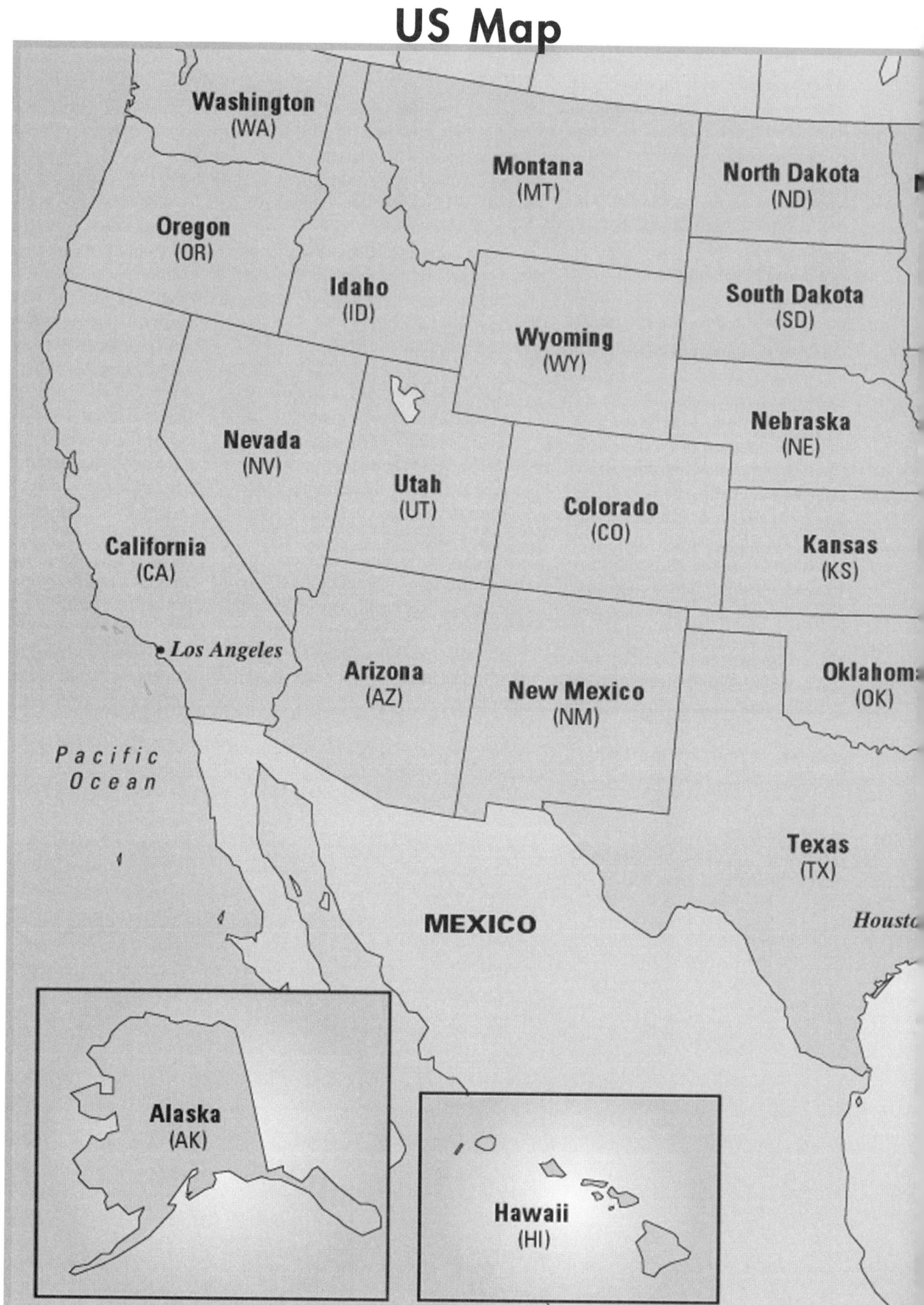

World Map

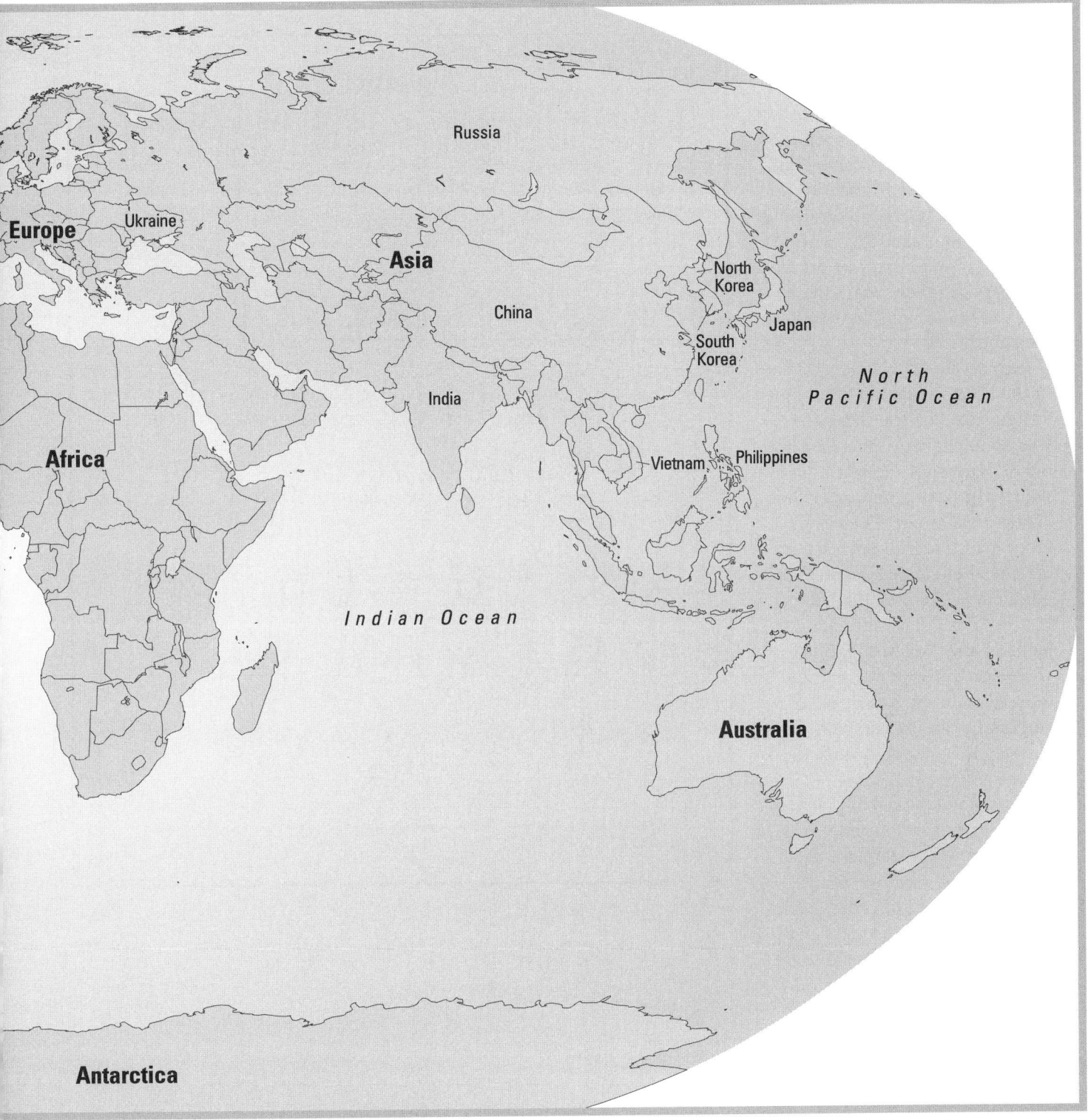

World Map 91

Alphabet

- Literacy-level learners benefit from periodic review of the alphabet. As you monitor learners' writing, refer to the alphabet on p. 90 in the student book any learners who are still having difficulty with letter formation. Indicate which letters you would like them to practice by writing them on a small piece of paper. Learners can then match the letters you wrote with the letters on the page.
- If learners have personal copies of the book, you can also assign writing practice for homework.
- Use the alphabet page as a listening activity after the warm-up units have been completed. Give learners paper clips, beans, or other markers. Call out a letter of the alphabet and ask learners to put their markers on the letters you say. Then have individual learners say the letters while a volunteer from the class writes the letters on the board. As a variation, learners can work with partners to say and identify the letters.
- For additional alphabet practice, divide learners into groups of three. Give each learner a paper on which you have written five to seven letters, out of order. Each group discusses the letters and then writes them in alphabetical order. Tell learners to check the alphabet page to see if they are correct.

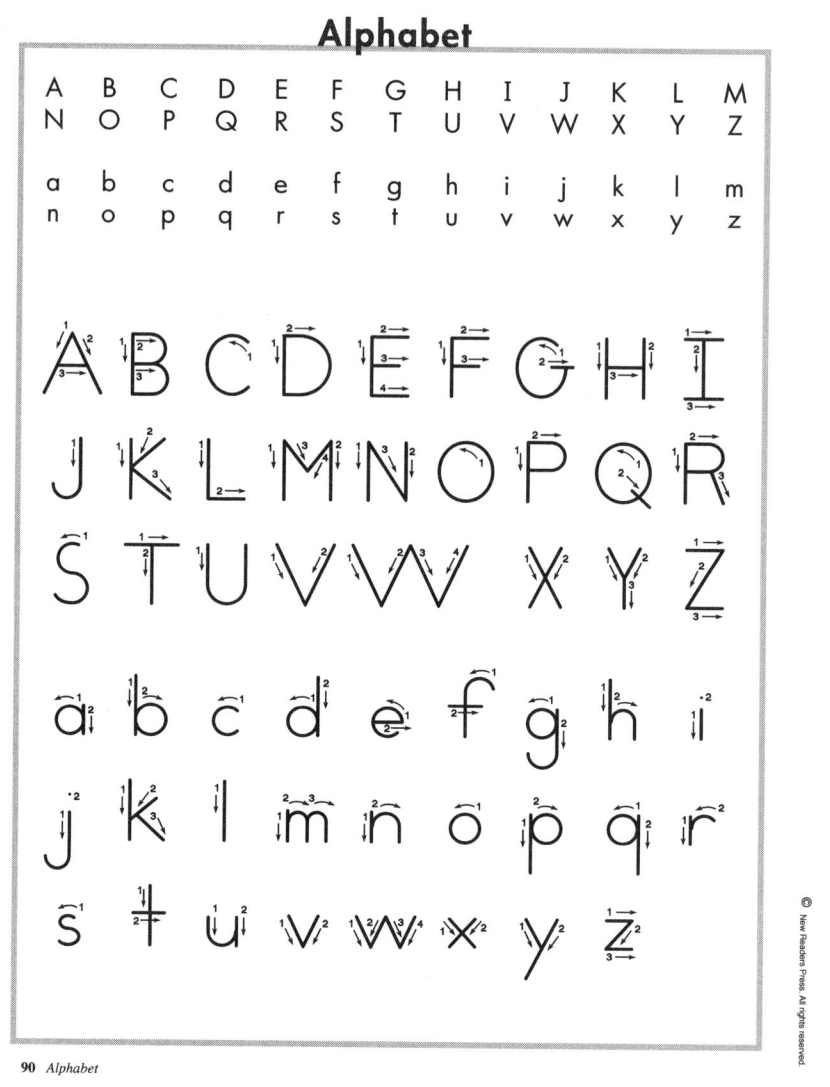

Numbers

- As the numbers are introduced in the units, refer learners to p. 91 in the student book for review. Give learners markers, call out numbers, and have learners put the markers on the numbers you say. As a variation, spell out number-words (e.g., t-w-e-n-t-y) and have learners put their markers on the correct numeral.
- Another variation is to use the numbers for dictation practice. Say a number and have learners write the number in words. To check their accuracy, have learners spell the number while you or a volunteer writes it on the board.
- Have learners make a number reference card to carry with them. Give learners 3 × 5 index cards. Divide the card into three equal columns. Leave room for writing numbers and words in each column. Divide each column into 10 rows. Write the numbers 1–10 in column one, 11–20 in column two, and 30–90 (by 10s), 100, and 1,000 in column three. Make a model of this card on the board or an overhead transparency.

Next have learners open their books to p. 91. Ask them to spell *one* as you write it next to the numeral 1 in the model on the board. Repeat for numbers two and three. Then have learners use the number page to complete the cards.

A variation is to use a computer to make business card–sized cards with the same information. Print the cards on card stock, laminate them, and give one to each learner to use as a pocket reference.

Numbers

0	1	2	3	4	5	6	7	8	9	10
zero	one	two	three	four	five	six	seven	eight	nine	ten

11	12	13	14	15	16	17	18	19	20
eleven	twelve	thirteen	fourteen	fifteen	sixteen	seventeen	eighteen	nineteen	twenty

21	22	23	24	25	26	27	28	29	30
twenty-one	twenty-two	twenty-three	twenty-four	twenty-five	twenty-six	twenty-seven	twenty-eight	twenty-nine	thirty

10	20	30	40	50	60	70	80	90	100
ten	twenty	thirty	forty	fifty	sixty	seventy	eighty	ninety	one hundred

200	300	400	500	600	700	800	900	1,000
two hundred	three hundred	four hundred	five hundred	six hundred	seven hundred	eight hundred	nine hundred	one thousand

0 1 2 3 4 5
6 7 8 9 10

Months, Days, and Time

Use the information on this page for periodic review after its content has been taught. Follow the directions for listening and dictation practice described for the alphabet and numbers.

For additional practice, do the following:
- Write the months and days on index cards.
- Cut apart the letters for each word and scramble them. Clip each set of letters together or put them in clear plastic zip-top bags.
- Divide learners into groups, give each group a set of three or four bags, and have them work together to put the letters in order to spell the names of months or days.
- Learners can check p. 92 to see if they are correct.

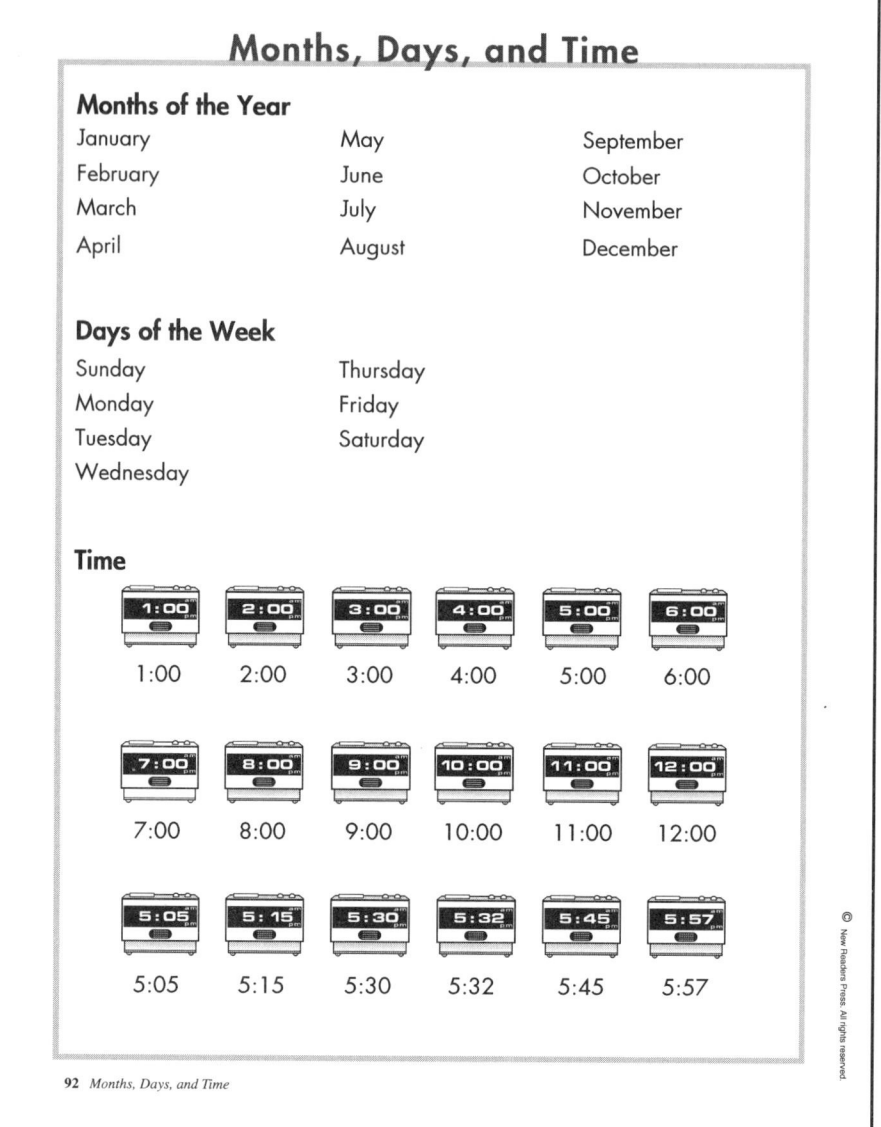

Money

Use the listening and dictation activities described for the alphabet and numbers. For additional practice do the following:

- Write various coin amounts on index cards. For example: write "three nickels" on one card and "two quarters, one dime, and three pennies" on another.
- Divide learners into pairs or groups of three and have them write the total dollar amount (e.g., $.15) for each card on a piece of paper.
- Then have them use p. 93 to see if they were correct.

Make a similar set of cards for paper money.

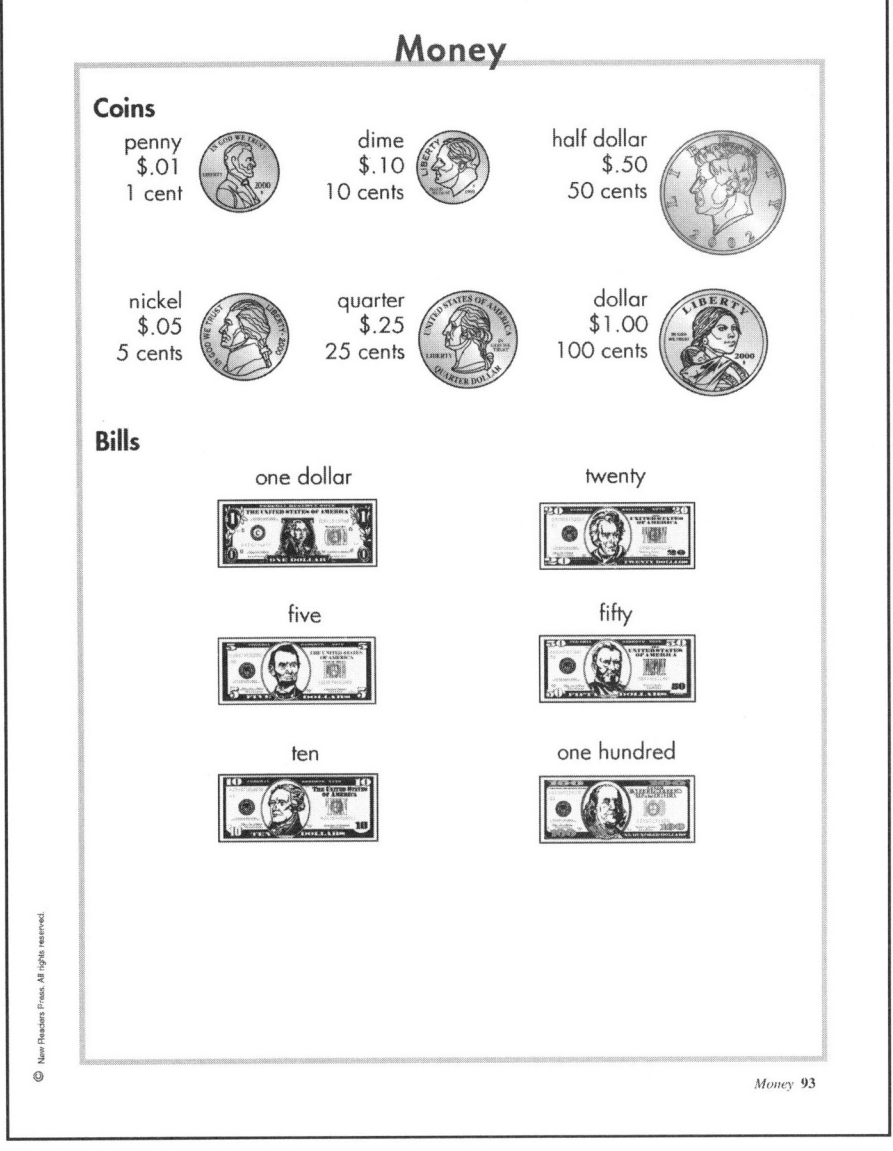

Topics

A
addresses, 38
alphabet, 11–14, 17–20, 90

B
birthdays, 58
body parts, 45

C
calling in sick, 44, 47, 50
cashing a check, 59
clothing, 75
colors, 21

D
dates, 58
days of the week, 48, 92

F
family, 33, 35
filling out forms, 27–28
food, 63, 65–66

G
giving change, 68

I
illnesses, 43, 45

L
letters
    lowercase, 17–20, 90
    uppercase, 11–14, 90

M
maps
    of the US, 86–87
    of the world, 88–89
meals, 66
men's and women's work, 67
money, 53, 55, 93
months of the year, 58, 92

N
names
    first, middle, and last, 14, 20, 27–28
newspaper ads, 70
numbers, 15, 29, 36, 49, 56, 91

P
places in the community, 60

S
school, 23, 25
signs in the community, 79

T
telephone numbers, 38
time, 49, 92
transportation, 78

W
weather, 73
weight
    pounds, 65

Language

A
ABC order, 11–14, 17–20

M
more and *less*, *plus* and *minus*, 68

N
nouns
    singular and plural, 29

P
polite expressions
    Excuse me, Please, Thank you, You're welcome, 39
    Nice day, 73
    Please repeat, 44
pronouns
    I, you, he, she, they, 40

T
titles
    Mr., Ms., Miss, Mrs., 35

V
verbs
    do/don't, does/doesn't, 75
    drive, ride, take, 78
    is with days, time, and health, 50
    need and *like*, 69

W
Wh- questions
    What? When? Where? Who?, 58

Workbook Answer Key

Warm-Up Unit A
Lesson 5
Exercise C
2. 5, five
3. 6, six

Exercise D
1 one
2 two
3 three
4 four
5 five
6 six
7 seven
8 eight
9 nine
10 ten

Warm-Up Unit B
Lesson 5
Exercise B
2. green
3. orange
4. purple
5. yellow

Exercise C
2. white
3. red
4. yellow
5. orange
6. blue

Unit 1
Lesson 1
Exercise A
2. Yes
3. No
4. Yes
5. No

Exercise B
2. school
3. pencil
4. student
5. pen
6. listen
7. classroom
8. point

Exercise C
2. a, 3. b, 4. f, 5. e, 6. g

Exercise E
2. classroom
3. listen
4. pencil
5. repeat
6. student
7. teacher

Exercise F
2. write
3. speak
4. listen
5. circle
6. read

Lesson 2
Exercise C
2. name
3. first
4. middle

Exercise D
2. Jimmy Sanders
3. Junko Sato
4. Hahn Emily Sara
5. John Jay Taylor

Exercise F
1 one
2 two
3 three
4 four
5 five
6 six
7 seven
8 eight
9 nine
10 ten
11 eleven
12 twelve
13 thirteen
14 fourteen
15 fifteen
16 sixteen
17 seventeen
18 eighteen
19 nineteen
20 twenty

Exercise G
2. three notebooks
3. ten schools
4. four teachers
5. twenty pencils

Exercise H
2. spell
3. last
4. middle
5. form
6. first

Unit 2
Lesson 1
Exercise A
2. daughter
3. mother
4. grandfather
5. grandmother
6. son

Exercise B
Column 2
grandfather
granddaughter
grandson
grandchild

Exercise C
2. She is Mrs. Garcia.
3. She is Miss Garcia.
4. He is Mr. Garcia.

Exercise E
2. man
3. parents
4. male
5. single
6. woman
7. female

Exercise G
parents
grandparents

Lesson 2
Exercise A
Ruben
husband
Mr.

Lela
grandmother
Mrs.
wife

Exercise B
3. 344-9685
4. 985-4209
5. 589-4306
6. 203-948-6059
7. 982-790-5654

Exercise C
2. zip code
3. state
4. e-mail address
5. city
6. street address

Exercise D
2. state
3. phone number
4. area code
5. zip code

Exercise E
2. Ben's last name is Lewis.
3. His address is 1621 Green Street, in Blue Lake, IL 60135.
4. His area code is 630.
5. His phone number is 555-8518.

Unit 3

Lesson 1
Exercise A
2. What's wrong?
3. She has a fever.
4. Excuse me. Please repeat.
5. A fever.
6. Oh, I see.

Exercise B
Dyna: What's wrong?
Nurse: She has a fever.
Dyna: Excuse me. Please repeat.
Nurse: A fever.
Dyna: Oh, I see.

Exercise C
2. clock
3. girl
4. head
5. nurse

Exercise E
2. nose
3. mouth
4. arm
5. foot
6. eye
7. ear
8. stomach
9. hand
10. leg

Exercise F
Head
ear
eye
nose

Body
arm
leg
hand

Exercise G
2. earache
3. backache
4. headache

Lesson 2
Exercise A
2. Yes. She's at home.
3. No. She's at home.
4. Yes. She's at home.
5. She's sick.

Exercise B
2. no
3. yes
4. no
5. yes
6. no
7. no
8. no
9. yes
10. no

Exercise C
2. 5:15
3. 12:45
4. 10:00
5. 9:15
6. 2:30
7. 4:45
8. 11:20
9. 8:00
10. 3:35

Exercise D
2. Thursday
3. Saturday
4. Monday
5. Wednesday
6. Friday
7. Thursday
8. Saturday
9. Tuesday
10. Sunday

Exercise E
Mon.
9:00-2:00
Tues.
total: 4
Wed.
1:00-4:00
Thurs.
total: 6
Fri.
10:00-3:30
Total for week: 23

Exercise F
2., 4. headache, backache
3. Thursday

Unit 4

Lesson 1
Exercise A
1. company name
2. amount
3. date
4. pay to
5. signature

Exercise C
2. dollar
3. nickel
4. penny
5. quarter

Exercise D
2. g
3. b
4. a
5. d
6. h
7. f
8. c
9., 10. j, e

Exercise E
10 dimes
20 nickels
4 quarters

Exercise F
2. d
3. a
4. b
5. e
6. f

Exercise G
2. Forty-five dollars and twenty-six cents
3. Thirty-two dollars and four cents

Lesson 2
Exercise A
1. Sixty-two and 90/100 dollars
3. Benjamin Lewis
4. 1234 Black St. Cambridge, MA 02139

Exercise B
2. b
3. i
4. k
5. g
6. j
7. c
8. l
9. f
10. a
11. h
12. e

Exercise C
2. 1/21/05
3. 6/9/92
4. 3/14/01
5. 11/11/87
7. October 4, 1967
8. June 2, 2003
9. August 24, 2002
10. April 8, 2007

Exercise D
One word
bank
pharmacy

Two words
gas station
post office

Exercise E
2. pharmacy
3. restaurant
4. supermarket

Exercise F
2. 7616 Oak St.
3. 7620 Oak St.
4. 7614 Oak St.

Unit 5

Lesson 1
Exercise A
2. refrigerator
3. bowl
4. table
5. cereal

Exercise B
2. The children are at the table.
3. The children have cereal.
4. Cereal is in the bowls.
5. They need milk.
6. The father says there's no milk!

Exercise C
1. e
2. c
3. d
4. f
5. a
6. b

Exercise D
2. 2 1/2 pounds
3. 1/2 pound

Exercise E
2. apples
3. milk
4. morning
5. cereal

Exercise F
Food
bread
carrots
rice

Drinks
milk
water

Exercise G
2. carrots
3. tea
4. juice
5. water
6. coffee

Exercise H
2. tomatoes
3. bananas
4. kitchen
5. rice
6. potatoes
7. rice
8. beans

Lesson 2
Exercise A
Ann and Greg have noodles, juice, beans.
They don't have cereal, oil, rice.

Exercise B
cereal, oil, rice

Exercise C
2. $.69
3. $3.19
4. $2.99
5. $.59
6. $8.99
7. $10.99
8. $.99

Exercise D
Greg's Shopping List
potatoes $.99
shrimp $10.99
total $15.17

Ann's Shopping List
beans $.69
rice $.89
bananas $.59
total $2.17
1. yes
2. no

Exercise E
```
A B C D E F G H I J K
C L B M N S H R I M P
A O R P Q R S T U V W
R R E P Q Z B B E E F
R O A D A P P L E S E
O T F D G H I J K L M N
T O P Q R S T U V W X
S Y Z A B C D E F G H
I J T O M A T O E S K
```

Exercise F
2. breakfast
3. pound
4. subtract
5. vegetables
6. morning

Unit 6

Lesson 1
Exercise A
2. cloudy, hot
3. rainy, warm
4. windy, cool
5. sunny, cold

Exercise C
2. skirt
3. shirt
4. gloves
5. shorts

Exercise D
2. raincoat
3. sunglasses

Exercise E
2. boots
3. snowy
4. cloudy
5. hot

Exercise F
2. a
3. d
4. f
5. e
6. c

Lesson 2
Exercise A
Photo 2: Ride with me tomorrow.
Photo 3: I hate the bus!
Photo 4: Tomorrow . . . the train!

Exercise B
2. drive
3. taxi
4. van
5. walk

Exercise C
Drive: van, bus, taxi
Take: van, bus, taxi
Ride: taxi, bicycle, train, bus

Exercise E
2. yes
3. no
4. yes

Exercise F
2. van
3. rides
4. department